My Sindh

A JOURNEY TO THE BELOVED HOMELAND

SHAKUNTALA BHARVANI

B&W

My Sindh

Published by black-and-white fountain

2 Flemington Terrace, Clover Village, Wanowari, Pune 411040, India

First edition April 2021

ISBN No 978-93-83465-26-2

ebook ISBN No 978-93-83465-24-8

Book design and cover design Veda Aggarwal

Editor: Saaz Aggarwal, with inputs from Mohindru Mirchandani

We are grateful to Zulfiqar Ali Kalhoro for the image of Satiyan jo Asthan with Lansdowne Bridge in the background, used on the cover.

http://sindhstories.wordpress.com

www.blackandwhitefountain.com

TO MY **IRB**,

WHOSE KNOWLEDGE AND LOVE OF SINDH

INSPIRED THIS BOOK.

FOR OUR CHILDREN,

VANDANA AND **DHIREN**, **VEDANT** AND **VEER.**

MAY THEY BE INSPIRED BY THESE STORIES

OF COURAGE, CONVICTION, AND COMMUNITY.

A note on the style used in this book

This book follows a language style on the spectrum between British and American usage, a middle ground generally considered acceptable in the globalization of the language. It chooses the idiomatic flow of contemporary English, lenient of an assortment that might include 'program', 'aeroplane', and others, as relevant or convenient. Logic, common sense, and the reader's comfort have been prioritized over finicky commitment to rules. In quotes from other sources embedded in the text, the style of the original has been retained, resulting in style inconsistencies from time to time. Captions of images display names of people from left to right. Abbreviations do not use full stops; double quotes "" have been used for conversation and single quotes '' for emphasis. While measurement uses the metric system, miles, pounds, and feet have been retained where contextually appropriate.

This is a book of history and nostalgia, and moves freely between the past and the present. Original place names, the ones she has been used to, mean a lot to the author, and the reader is requested to excuse the frequent and inconsistent use of 'Calcutta' for 'Kolkata', 'Bombay' for 'Mumbai' and so on. Sindh was called Scinde, Sinde, and Sindy by the British. In this book, the contemporary spelling Sindh is used. Hyderabad, Sindh, in most instances, is just Hyderabad.

Italics is always a tricky business, and many Indian words likely to be familiar to readers of this book have been left in straight face, as to italicize them would be to interrupt the smooth flow of reading. Many Sindhi words, however, have been presented in a font that simulates the Sindhi script, with a view to nudging readers towards their heritage, and meanings have been provided within brackets or dashes. There are, however, quite a few non-English words and phrases that have been left untranslated ('Chikni Chachi' is an example) because of the challenge of providing sufficient meaning and context in a short space. In such cases, readers are requested to consult Google if required.

The author of this book has been a professor of English for more than four decades, and in this book she has used a conversational style spiked with humour and irony. An astonishing number of sentences begin with 'And' and 'But'! However, her writing is also strewn with literary allusions. With respect and affection for her young readers, she has tried to explain each one in the course of the text, but here, too, readers may want to reach out to the internet for further explanation.

Contents

A SPATIAL REPRESENTATION OF OUR LOST HOMELAND, SINDH, MARKING SOME OF THE PLACES MENTIONED IN THIS BOOK. THE RIVER INDUS IS REPRESENTED BY THE LINE OF FISH FLOWING THROUGH THE IMAGE.
IMAGE COURTESY SAAZ AGGARWAL

1. Crocodiles, camels, and Quetta

My brother Ajit, who is just two or three years older than I am, has a fantastic memory and remembers several incidents which took place during our childhood of which I have not the vaguest remembrance. Sometimes I wonder if he is making up stories just to impress me. For suddenly he will come up with something like, "You know what happened to me in Quetta when I was three years old? I ate five pounds of grapes at one sitting and then I was sick for five days."

I try and believe him because, after all these years, I know that much of what he says is true. His memory is extraordinary! Yes, Quetta did have the most juicy, mouth-watering grapes. And not just grapes but all varieties of fruit: sweet rosy apples, plums, peaches, pomegranates, apricots, cherries and the incomparable sarda, a variety of melon, that my parents often spoke of in later years, with nostalgic longing. It is not without reason that Quetta was referred to as the fruit basket of Sindh. But how could a child of three have ever eaten five pounds of grapes in one go?

Ajit was a pre-Partition child, born in Karachi in 1942, and he has vivid memories of St Patrick's School which he attended very briefly. He remembers being told that he was born in a maternity home run by a Malayali lady, Dr Anna Thomas, on Bunder Road in Karachi. And he even remembers the name of the steamer in which our family sailed from Karachi to Jam Khambalia: SS Sonavati, when raging riots broke out and there was no choice for Hindus but to flee the newly-formed country named Pakistan. He remembers my father explaining to my grandmother that travelling by train was risky because Hindus trying to escape on trains were being slaughtered or robbed.

He also has vivid memories of our arrival at Jam Khambhalia, a port in Gujarat, where we stayed at a guesthouse belonging to a Gujarati family my father had known and worked with in Quetta. He can recall the railway station close by, and the durwan who used to sit at the entrance. And then, according to his story, he went and met the old durwan on a visit to Gujarat a few years ago and surprisingly the durwan recognized him! Apparently the ninety-year-old former durwan said, "Of course I remember you, sahib. You climbed that tree there and fell and broke your arm and then you screamed and cried. I carried you in my arms and walked around asking everyone who your parents were. There were so many refugees arriving at the dharamshala every day!"

Anyway, to come to the point, I visited Ajit recently. He continues to live in Calcutta, where my parents settled after Partition, and where we grew up.

Only a small percentage of the Sindhis evicted from Sindh settled in Calcutta. For my father in the tea-trading business, it seemed a logical choice, and his tea business flourished. In those days, Calcutta was India's largest centre for tea trading and auctions, and the family prospered. Our parents ensured that we four siblings received an excellent education. Ashok, the eldest, is a respected civil engineer and consulted on the value of properties by government authorities and courts. His book *Valuation Principles and Procedures* is a scholarly work that bridges the theoretical and practical aspects of real-estate valuation.

Ajit, a year younger and the quintessential Sindhi entrepreneur, runs the Harvard House chain of schools. Both live in Calcutta. I chose to become an academic, and my sister Mira, the baby of the family, is now the eminent Bombay gynaecologist and obstetrician Dr Mira Raisinghaney, well known as a fertility expert.

I had taken the 6am flight from Mumbai's Chhatrapati Shivaji airport and arrived at what I still thought of as Dum Dum in Kolkata, despite its glamorous reincarnation as Netaji Subhas Chandra International Airport, at around 9am. Ashok was away in the USA visiting his son, and Ajit picked me up. We reached Ajit's Theatre Road residence and I decided to change, have breakfast and refresh myself with a short nap, as I had woken very early that morning. But hardly had I drunk a glass of water when Ajit marched into my room and enthusiastically announced, "Come, come! We are going on a picnic!"

"What?" I asked, thinking that, with the sound of the aeroplane engine still buzzing in my ears, I must have heard wrong.

"We are going on a picnic," he repeated.

"Ajit! I woke up at 3am to catch this 6 o'clock flight. I've just put my feet up. Don't forget I'm a senior citizen! I need to rest."

"But tomorrow I'm busy at the schools and won't have time. We must go to the zoo, let's leave right now!"

I was astonished. Could this be dementia? Or perhaps a joke?

Slowly, placatingly, so that even someone who may have lost his mental balance would understand, I said, "Ajit, our children are scattered around the world, like good Sindhis! Let's take them all to the famous Alipore Zoo when they visit Calcutta next. What are we, two old fuds, going to do in the zoo? And that too in this scorching afternoon heat of May?"

I tried to sound as reasonable and logical as I could. Sometimes my brother comes up with crazy ideas, and I had to keep my cool! I remember once, when we were little, there was an earthquake and he had quietly crept under the bed.

After the tremors subsided, my mother nearly went berserk because he was just ten and we couldn't find him anywhere. It was our house help who suddenly spotted him, fast asleep under his bed! When my mother interrogated him, he calmly explained that it was the safest place during an earthquake.

"But," said Mother, "the bed and the ceiling would have fallen on you."

"No," he insisted adamantly, "Only the bed would have fallen on me."

In my most sisterly voice, I explained that I was tired and needed a little rest.

"No," he said stubbornly, "We have to go just now. I've made the driver wait, and there is a box of sandwiches and some of your favourite kathi kabab rolls from Nizam's already in the car. Just get into your walking shoes and we're all set."

There was no way out. I was convincing myself that it couldn't possibly be dementia. Ajit is a genius with crossword puzzles and Sudoku. There is nothing he can't solve. I had recently sent him a large collection of crosswords clipped from various magazines, and he had raced through them all in a week and asked for more.

So there we were at the zoo, in the blistering afternoon heat of May. After buying the tickets at the entrance, my brother strode ahead purposefully, saying, "Meet me after an hour near the camel enclosure. There is a bench under a tree near it."

I wandered around aimlessly. It is not easy to get up at 3am and then spend the afternoon looking at monkeys and donkeys. I remembered when my daughter Vandana was four and we were visiting Calcutta, how she loved to stop and watch the monkeys. In those days, visitors would thoughtlessly hand cigarettes to the monkeys and, to our horror, enjoy the sight of monkeys puffing on them. I stood and looked at the monkeys, glad that such behaviour is now strictly forbidden, and wishing I was home on a comfortable mattress with a pillow under my head. Some of the monkeys were resting. Ah, how I envied them, and wished I was a monkey too. At the appointed time, I arrived at the camel enclosure, and found Ajit standing there. Staring in sheer ecstasy at the shaggy four-legged sandy-coloured creatures, and admiring their elongated necks.

"Look!" he said excitedly, when he finally noticed that I had joined him, "Look at that little baby. It can't be more than a few months old but see how confidently it is walking."

I looked at Ajit. Something was definitely wrong with him. Was this what dementia looked like? An elderly bespectacled man, perspiration streaming down his face, gazing in rapture at camels?

"Look at their beautiful long eyelashes. Did you know they have long eyelashes to protect them from the sand flying into their eyes in the desert and ..."

"Ok let's hurry up. I read all that in a geography textbook at school."

Ajit looked at me reproachfully. "Well, Nana told me that. He said that a camel could go without water for a long time, and that baby camels learn to walk very early."

How on earth could Nana, our maternal grandfather, have told him all this? Surely not from the grave. Our Nana had passed away soon after Partition, unable to bear the privation of life in cramped and dirty refugee camps, and preoccupied with the dilemma of supporting his family's daily needs. In Sindh he had been a zamindar of Bhiria, a village in Nawabshah district. A dignified landlord who lived in style and comfort.

"Don't you remember?" he continued.

"No, I don't. Nana passed away when I was a kid. How do you expect me to remember anything?"

"The best riding camels are brought from Mikran, and their speed when well trained is almost incredible, the pace being a long trot."
From *Personal Observations on Sindh* by Thomas Postans (1843) p109

"There used to be so many camels in his fields. And Nana would always take me for a ride on his favourite one when we visited him in Bhiria. And all his peasants and workers bowed down and greeted us. Don't you remember?" He asked again.

"No, I don't."

"Of course you won't! But I do. Nana also told me that the Sindhi camels are better looking than the Arab ones! And there are some parts of Sindh so sandy that you can travel only on camel-back. Horses would slip in that sand."

"Ok," I said, tugging at his arm. "Shall we go home now?" He trudged on relentlessly, ignoring me. Obviously, our visit to the zoo was not over yet!

"We will now go and see the 'magormachh'," he admonished, pronouncing the word for crocodile in the accent of a good Bengali bhadralok, one who has grown up in the city of Calcutta. For Ajit speaks Bangla better than he speaks Sindhi. This is the case with most of us Sindhis: we pick up local languages but cannot speak our own mother tongue. This is, of course, because our own native land was lost to us forever after Partition.

Looking at my tired face, he reprimanded me sternly, "You look half asleep!"

"Of course I'm fagged out," I responded petulantly and asked, with as much sarcasm as I could muster," did Nana take you for a crocodile ride as well?"

Ajit ignored my comment and hurried purposefully towards the crocodile enclosure. "See," he said, when I caught up with him, "I never got a chance to visit Mangho Pir because of Partition. But Nana often told me about the crocs there."

"You should go for a ride on a croc," I repeated, feeling quite perverse.

"What did you say? A ride on a croc? You are always trying to be witty! For a change now, listen to me and think of all that you missed because of Partition!"

"Ok, let's see the crocs and get going."

"About 15 kilometres from Karachi," Ajit persisted, "lies the shrine of the saint Mangho. He arrived in Sindh from Baghdad, one of the many who fled the marauding

Feeding the Rajah
From *Kurrachee: Past, Present and Future* by Alexander F Baillie (1880)

Mongols in the thirteenth century. As the story goes, an enormous crocodile appeared to protect him. He is 15 feet long and is called Mor Sahib. These days there are hundreds of crocs there – all supposedly the progeny of Mor Sahib!"

"Maybe you could do croc farming!" I replied, rolling my eyes. "I hear crocodile-skin handbags and wallets are in great demand and you being such a hotshot Sindhi entrepreneur could ..."

"Don't be profane! The croc is the totem of Mangho Pir, and these crocs are the manifestations of the presence of the saint. Both Hindus and Muslims worship there. Didn't I tell you that I'm part of a Sufi band in Kolkata?"

I was already weary at the sight of these odious reptiles and the thought of hundreds of them was making me nauseous. I hurried out into the open and stood under the shade of a tree, half listening as he continued: "The hot springs at the site of the shrine, dear sister, would have cured that rash on your arm and your exhaustion. That is, if you had faith!"

I was already heading for the exit gate to wait for him

MAGAR TALAO OR ALLIGATOR TANK
FROM *DRY LEAVES FROM YOUNG EGYPT* BY EDWARD EASTWICK (1849)

when he called me back, "Wait, wait! I must have some dab pani. The cream of the dab reminds me somewhat of the sweet creamy sardas we used to have in Quetta!"

"Yes of course," I muttered mutinously under my breath, "I do believe that nothing here can ever compare with the fruit of Quetta, whether fresh or dry." But always the dutiful younger sister, I walked back and enjoyed the coconut water with Ajit before we went home, and I finally got a chance to rest.

2. The Salt Hedge

AND VARIOUS OTHER DIVISIONS

In the 1870s, travellers could not walk from the western part of India across to the east. Anyone who tried to, would encounter a barrier and be forced to halt. Made of babool, bamboo, prickly pear, and other thorny local shrubs, this was a thick blockade which could not be crossed. When a break appeared – there stood a chowki. Travellers intent on going through, would be interrogated by police and customs officials. They would be searched, and if found to be carrying salt, the officials would pounce in glee, levying fines and taxes.

I had heard about the Great Wall of China, the Berlin Wall, Hadrian's Wall and even Trump's Mexican Wall! These walls and barricades were intended to ward off invaders, enemies, ruffians and looters. So it was interesting to come across a book called *The Great Hedge of India* by Roy Moxam, which describes a great hedge erected in India. Two thousand miles long, the hedge was planned and created by our erstwhile colonial rulers. It was conceived not to protect the gold and silver or objects which they usurped, such as the sword of Tipu Sultan or the Kohinoor diamond, but to prevent salt from being smuggled.

Salt is freely available in large parts of India – along the coast, from the sea, from our six inland salt lakes and our magnificent Rann of Kachchh. Today, India is the third-largest salt producing country in the world, after China and the USA. But in 1872, Moxam reports, more than 14,000 staff – Indians, I can only presume! – were employed to patrol the line and apprehend salt smugglers. Because salt, in British India, could only be traded against a high tax.

Moxam came across the annual reports of the India Inland Customs Department in which the hedge 'impassable to man or beast' is described in meticulous detail:

> The dry hedge is chiefly composed of dwarf Indian plum ... But in most places, material is procured at a cost of enormous labour: white ants and jungle fires perpetually destroy the dry hedge, at which our work is ceaseless; while storms and whirlwinds, especially in the plain of the Punjab, carry away whole furlongs and even, occasionally, miles of it in an hour. In its most perfect form, the hedge is a live one, from 10 to 14 feet in height, and 6 to 12 feet thick, composed of closely clipped thorny trees and shrubs, among which the babool, Indian plum, the carounda, the prickly pear and the thuer (euphorbia) are the most numerous.

The salt tax

The Imperial government, always on the lookout for ways and means to make money, discovered that India's abundant salt could be used profitably to the advantage of the Imperial Exchequer by imposing excise and other duties on its sale, and later on its production. They also introduced their own Cheshire and Liverpool salt at a lower price, which made it attractive to buy. And salt became such an important source of revenue that it was decided to build a hedge to prevent it being smuggled across the Inland Customs Line. It is interesting to read the figures recorded by Alexander Baillie in his book *Karachi: Past, Present and Future* (1880), which are self-explanatory and indicative of the profits reaped by the British:

Gross receipts from salt amounted to	...	Rs 423,087
Expenditure amounted to	...	Rs 27,526
Net income (profit)	...	Rs 395,560

So while the colonial rulers earned a good income, the common man paid a steep price. And this was not the only drawback: a large supply of the consumption of salt in Karachi was derived from patches of salt scattered over the surrounding countryside and was produced by peasants who gained a living from its manufacture. They were able to sell this salt in the local bazaars at 10 annas for a camel load, which would have weighed four to five hundred pounds. But since these patches had been brought under the control of the British government, it was a loss to the labour as their earnings and livelihood came to a standstill.

Colonial villainy

During the Indian freedom movement, one of the biggest protests was conducted against this salt tax. As a child, I often heard my parents talk about Mahatma Gandhi and the Dandi Salt March of 1930. They related this great historic protest to me, as a reminder that I should not waste salt. Even when I put too much salt into a glass of water to gargle, they would caution me that half a teaspoonful was sufficient. The frugality surprised me, because when we went to the New Market in Calcutta to shop for groceries, my mother would purchase a seer – an old measure which amounts to a little less than one kilogram – of salt in a paper bag, as this was in the late 1950s, the era before plastic. And she would pay just one anna for it.

When I reminded my mother about this and told her that salt was inexpensive, all she said was, "Salt is God-given, and you shouldn't waste anything that is God-given. And you don't know how expensive salt had become in the olden days."

I was reminded of the 'olden days' quite often by my parents, and I sometimes thought they were referring to the Stone Age or some pre-historic medieval period. As I grew older, I realized they were referring to life in Sindh before Partition, and the heavy taxes levied on salt during those days of British rule.

The greed and villainy of the British are clearly documented in the matter of cloth production too. Shashi Tharoor in his inimitable picturesque style describes how the new rulers "smashed the thumbs" of Indian handloom weavers, broke their looms, and imposed tariffs and duties on their cloth and products.

Wrote Popati Hiranandani in *Sindhis, a Scattered Treasure*:

> Almost all travellers and historians confirm the fact that Sindh mainly exported its products, especially the textiles. When the British came to Sindh, they were astonished to see the art and skill of colour-blending of the Sindhi weavers. There are nostalgic memories of the ladies wearing their upper garment (chaddar) of Amberu – a rainbow coloured material with bright red and yellow hues blended together. They wore pyjamas of Soosi – a dress material with bright violet background and white stripes. The people of Northern Sindh were very proud of producing Rohri silk. Ladies of those days cherished the wish of having a kurta of Kanweez – a material having two shades of colours blended together. There were innumerable varieties of dress materials in Sindh and the durability of those textiles was such that the mother-in law preserved her dresses and the dress materials which she got in her trousseau, as precious heirlooms for her daughters-in-law.

I remember my own grandmother wearing a chaddar of the finest white woven muslin at my wedding. I was surprised, as this was the first time I had seen it, and when I asked her, she told me that she had been saving it to wear at my wedding!

These were the kind of beautiful heirloom fabrics that the British rulers hampered the production of. They took away our cotton and shipped it to England. What would later be called 'The Industrial Revolution' had just begun. They were setting up mills and began machine-producing cloth in Lancashire, and we in India became its buyers and wearers. And then, as Tharoor concludes, "Our native weavers became beggars."

Gandhi's salt march

One of the permanent reminders of the salt atrocity of the British is an event of history that most Indian school children are familiar with, the Dandi March. In 1930, Gandhi, by then already seen as a leader of our freedom movement and referred to as 'Mahatma', the great soul, walked with a group of his followers from his Sabarmati Ashram to Dandi beach in south Gujarat. He was joined by some Sindhi young men and women too, including the senior Congress leader JB Kripalani. As they walked, more joined in. An elderly rheumatic uncle of my father's had also sworn to join Gandhi's march but due to his persistent knee pain and heart problem, regretfully relinquished the idea!

Thousands followed Gandhi to defy the British, and as Gandhi knelt down to say a prayer, he also picked up a fistful of salt. The crowds cheered and followed suit. People from the surrounding coastal areas of Surat and Karachi also began to pick up fistfuls of salt to defy the inhuman taxation on a natural and free product of our own oceans and soil.

Economists point out that even when the price of salt continues to rise, it is one of those essential commodities that people will continue to buy. Everyone needs salt – rich man, poor man, beggarman, thief – everyone! And its uses are infinite. Salt is an essential ingredient in the cooking of food, preservation of pickles, curing of meat and fish, manufacture of soap, melting of ice in winter when the roads get frozen, preparation of washing soda and baking soda! If you dip an inverted glass into a plateful of salt, it forms a thin rim of silvery salt around the edge. Fill the glass and enjoy your margarita – as IRB and I so often did!

Loon Mouan ceremony

And salt is not essential only for food and drink. What would our Sindhi marriage ceremony be without salt? The post-marriage auspicious ritual 'Loon Mouan' is a symbolic commitment to cordiality between the new bride and her new family. When she steps into her new home after the marriage ceremony, a thaal filled with salt is placed in front of her. She picks up a handful of salt and puts it in her husband's hands. He passes it back into her hands. This ceremony of exchanging handfuls of salt, called **Jattara** by some, is performed with all the other relatives who are present, and represents a happy and long-lasting relationship.

So, if you visit the Rann of Kachchh, carry an empty sack and bring it back filled with salt for your marriage ceremony! To witness our Rann – Sindh lies just across it – by sunlight or by moonlight, in the evening or in the afternoon, is akin to witnessing one of the greatest wonder of wonders. This salty desert shimmers like a twinkling carpet of silver. It is loaded with hundreds of millions of tons of good-quality glistening salt, a natural product of our Sindhu River. There are 3,000 square miles of salt-encrusted sand going

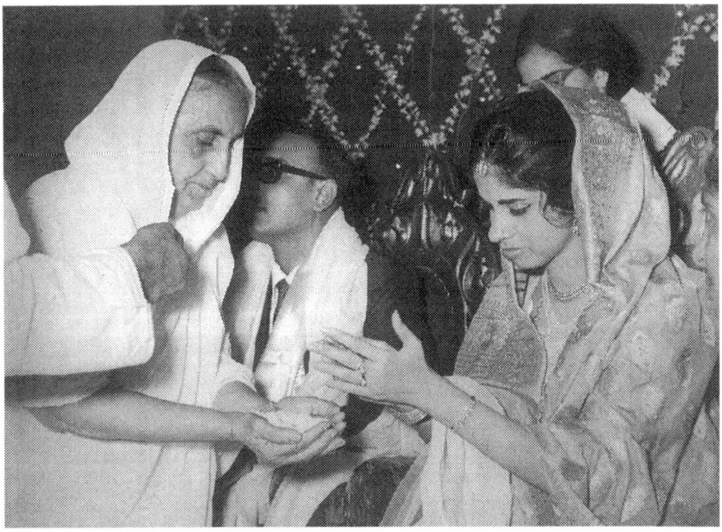

Shakuntala Bharvani performs 'Loon Mouan' at her wedding.
Bombay, 1968

shimmer-shimmer, waiting to be picked up. And don't forget to exchange handfuls of salt with your friends, and maybe your enemies too!

3. How to build an empire

IN A FEW EASY STEPS

The British were planners par excellence. That quality undoubtedly contributed to making them rulers of a vast empire, one on which, as they liked to boast, "the sun never set". While reading about their conquest of Sindh, I came across some fascinating and inspiring facts. Facts from which we should all learn lessons.

The first lesson I learnt was that several Brits who lived and served in India were fluent in the Indian languages. They compiled dictionaries and even translated works written in the Indian languages into various European languages. And several of them knew Hindustani. Officers posted in Sindh knew how to read, write and speak Sindhi. Sir Ivan Taunton could carry on a conversation fluently in Sindhi. Both Richard Burton and Edward Eastwick's linguistic abilities in several Oriental languages including Sindhi and Hindustani are evident in their work. Eastwick had mastered the Sindhi language so meticulously that he even wrote a book on Sindhi grammar.

Sometimes they went around in disguise and spoke in Sindhi to 'spy' and garner information about plots being hatched against them. The case of Richard Burton is the most prominent, but there were several others too.

This made me think: "Why have I never learnt to read and write my own mother tongue? I can speak it reasonably well, but is that enough? Thinking of the British rulers who mastered Sindhi inspired me to start studying my mother tongue in my senior years.

My second lesson was that the British conquest of India combines History, Military Tactics and Management. As an academic for more than forty years, it has led me to frame a marvelous inter-disciplinary course which could be offered under any one of these titles:

- Golden Tips to Transform a Small Business into an Empire
- Game Plan: Start Small Think Big
- Don't Give an Inch and you Won't Lose a Mile

All three titles are relevant to the strategy the British adopted in their conquest of Sindh!

Ascent of the British encroachment

When I began reading about Sindh, I learnt that the East India Company had set up a trading factory in Lower Sindh in 1635. They closed it in 1662, and then again ran it from 1758 to 1775.

Like most of us who read about factories, the image in my mind was of a place of production with machines and various appliances. However, when I started reading historical documents about the factories set up by the East India Company, I learnt to my surprise that these factories were more in the nature of townships. Inside a fortified exterior, there was a vast complex of warehouses, residential quarters, offices, sometimes a small library, a school, and in most cases a church or prayer room as well.

Line of March: a regiment of the British army enters Sindh

Those Brits made themselves quite comfortable inside their factories!

When IRB and I visited Chennai in 2010, we made a special trip to the factory that had been established in Fort St George. It now houses a number of government offices and some exhibition halls. The Anglican Church inside the factory is still maintained well, and there we saw the Church Register. Turning the pages, we saw the registration of the marriages of Robert Clive and Governor Elihu Yale. Both these marriages had been solemnized in the prayer room there!

Initially, the factories of the East India Company were commercial enterprises, and during this early period, the Company's interest centred solely around commerce. But after 1775, with the decline in trade, particularly in the area of textile manufacture, the Company removed its established factories, and focused its efforts on the systematic acquisition of power, prestige and a passage through Sindh to the lands beyond.

Dealing with Napoleon

The British first became concerned that another power might get the better of them with the rise of the ambitious Napoleon Bonaparte, between 1804 and 1814. They realised that he intended to invade India with an army, and that they had to act swiftly. The North-West Frontier, bordering Afghanistan and Balochistan, served more

These images were drawn by a British officer c1843

as a passage to invaders than a barrier. Their fears were intensified with the 1807 Treaty of Tilsit between France, Russia and Prussia, which had the motive of destroying Britain's commerce by closing all their ports to British trading ships. This put the British on guard and they contrived a policy of recruiting conspirators which would enable them to be kept informed of moves and alliances which their competitors might be forging.

Dealing with the Sindhis

Amirs of Sind
from *Dry Leaves from Young Egypt* by Edward Eastwick (1849)

The first 'mole' sent to Sindh was Nathaniel Crowe.

He was sent in 1800 by the Government of Bombay, to Hyderabad. His mission was purely political, but it was made out to be a commercial appointment. Sindh was ruled at the time from Hyderabad by a Baloch tribe called the Talpurs. Their early rule was known as the first 'chaaryaari' or 'rule of four friends'.

Crowe met Mir Fateh Ali, chief of the 'chaaryaar', in a friendly manner. The Talpurs suspected the British of ulterior motives, but Crowe assured them that he desired only to remove any previous discord, and pointed out to them the advantages of a British alliance. If a factory was permitted to be set up, it would increase the wealth of Sindh and also ward off Zaman Shah, king of Afghanistan, from eyeing Sindhi territory. In addition, it would thwart the ambitions of the French.

Though Mir Fateh Ali was favourably inclined, the three junior Mirs of his team of four brothers, were suspicious. They insisted that Fateh Ali expel Crowe, and he had to leave Sindh speedily.

Mir Fateh Ali Khan died in 1802 and was replaced by his brother, Mir Ghulam Ali Khan. Ghulam had previously been opposed to the British connection but now, fearing another Afghan invasion, he sent an envoy to the governor's office in Bombay. They did not receive him, but Bombay had received intelligence that envoys from Sindh had already left for Persia to negotiate with the Shah of Iran. The Persians would aid the Mirs, and in return the Mirs would cooperate with the Shah in case of an Afghan threat. There were also rumours of friendly French footfalls on Sindh soil.

This news alerted the British Government of India, which realized that nothing should be overlooked, and an emissary should be sent to Sindh immediately to demand re-establishment of a factory. The main aim of the emissary would be to study and gauge the political situation.

With this in mind, David Seton was sent from Britain as Resident to Sindh in 1808. Seton agreed to some of the proposals of the Mirs. He felt that his actions were in keeping with the mission allotted to him: to re-establish relations with Sindh and to undermine Russian, French, and Persian influence at all costs. But the British government felt that he had committed himself too far and he was recalled.

Nicholas Hankey Smith came next and tactfully revoked the earlier agreement but failed to make any new arrangement as the Mirs felt a revised agreement would tie them to the British without giving them any reciprocal advantage.

After Smith's mission, the relationship between Britain and Sindh deteriorated because the Mirs wished to extend their territory to Kachchh and, with Britain defending it against them, a clash occurred between British and Sindh forces. Mountstuart Elphinstone, who was Governor of Bombay between 1819 and 1827, prepared to take military action but met with disapproval from Governor-General Lord Moira who ordered:

"War with Sindh would be an evil as tending to involve us in disputes, jealousies, enmities, intrigues, negotiations, wars and incalculable embarrassment in the countries beyond the Indus."

So a compromise was reached, and a treaty was signed with the Mirs on 9 November 1820, promising friendship between the two parties. After this, all was quiet for a decade. Napoleon had been defeated and the Brits could now turn their attention to Russia.

Dealing with the Russians

In the late 1820s, two books appeared which impressed Lord Ellenborough, President of the Board of Control, and later Governor General of India from 1842 to 1844. The first one was Dr James Burnes' book *A Narrative of a Visit to the Court of Sindh* which described the doctor's visit to attend to the medical needs of the ailing Talpur Mir, Murad Ali Khan. His visit to what was seen as a forbidden frontier was of special interest to the British government, eagerly waiting and watching for an opportunity to get a foothold into the land of the Mirs. These books by colonial writers sometimes give colourful real-life glimpses of their journeys. James Burnes talks about "100 camels on the beach laden with ghee" travelling from Sindh to Kachchh!

The other book was *On the Designs of Russia* by Colonel De Lacey Evans. These books created in the minds of the colonial rulers a strong sense of a forthcoming struggle for power against the Russians on the Indus.

Dealing with Raja Ranjit Singh

The ambitious Ellenborough resolved to obtain full information of Russian activities in the countries between the Caspian and the Indus. Previous attempts to survey the river had been frustrated by the Mirs, who guarded their territory fiercely, fully aware that British knowledge of the river would invite intrusion.

But Ellenborough found a covert way of disguising British intentions: Raja Ranjit Singh had sent a coronation present to William IV. Ellenborough now proposed to reciprocate by sending him a return gift of one dray horse and four dray mares. The horses were taken from Bombay through Kachchh. To reach Lahore, they would have to be accompanied up the Indus to Lahore by an emissary. This emissary would have every opportunity to survey the river!

Alexander Burnes, elder brother of Dr James Burnes, was entrusted with the task of delivering the cargo of five beautiful dray horses and a carriage as a gift from the King of Great Britain to Raja Ranjit Singh (who, according to some sources, had no use for them whatsoever).[1]

With this heavy cargo, the journey through Sindh and the surrounding areas was slow, and Burnes, supplied with surveying instruments and ample funds, was able to closely study the terrain and the sacred river of Sindh without raising any suspicion. The cavalcade also carried gifts which would please the Mirs and make the passage easier through their territories:

> "... a gun, a brace of pistols, a gold watch, two telescopes, a clock, some English shawls and clothes, elegant cut-glass candlesticks ... some Persian works beautifully lithographed in Bombay and a map of the world and Hindoostan..."[2]

The cavalcade started from Kachchh on 21 January 1831, and made two attempts to land in Sindh but the Mirs would not let the mission proceed, proffering excuses such as the presence of bandits and the lack of water in the Indus. Eventually, facing threats from the British that a military demonstration would be set up if the cargo was not allowed to continue its journey, the Mirs relented. Observing the contingent proceeding on their journey down the river, a Sindhi Syed was reported to have remarked prophetically, "Alas! Sindh is gone, now that the English have seen the river."[3]

---

1 *Origin of the Sikh Power in the Punjab* compiled by Henry T Prinsep 1834. GH Huttman Military Orphan Press p152-158

2 *Travels into Bokhara and A Voyage on the Indus* (Vol 3) by Alexander Burnes,1834, p 46

3 Introduction to *Memoirs of Seth Naomul Hotchand of Karachi* by Hamida Khuhro

Edward Backhouse Eastwick records another conversation with an elderly Balochi, who asked him, "Why do you go far from home to take other people's countries from them?"

Eastwick replied, "The Turks do the same."

"Ah! You wish to be such oppressors as the Turks," said the man bitterly, and told Eastwick not to talk to him anymore.

Burnes studied everything minutely and made detailed notes. And he recorded other interesting details about Sindh as well.[4]

> ... the river fish are likewise abundant ... of these the most remarkable is the 'pulla' ... delicious in flavour and only found in the four months that precede the swell of the river ... the staple production of the delta of the Indus is rice ... it is to be had of many different kinds ... Bajra and all other Indian grains are raised. From extensive plantations of cane, 'goor', a coarse kind of sugar is produced ... saltpetre is found in the delta, but it is not exported, though formerly an object of commerce to the East India Company.

Indeed, one of the chief attractions of Sindh was its saltpetre, a rare commodity and much in demand for the production of gunpowder.

End of the first Chaaryaari

Over time, the four Mirs of the chaaryaari died: Mir Fateh Ali in 1810, Mir Ghulam Ali a year later, then Mir Karam Ali and finally the youngest, who had been treated by Dr James Burnes, Mir Murad Ali. By this time, much of India was under British rule and the Great Game – as the political and diplomatic confrontation between Great Britain and

4 *Travels into Bokhara and A Voyage on the Indus* (Vol 3) by Alexander Burnes,1834, p 46

Russia over Afghanistan and neighbouring territories in Central and South Asia is often referred to – was in full swing. The British had been hawkishly eyeing Sindh for its wealth and strategic position, and were making inroads with new agreements. They were also fanning the seeds of discontent within the ranks of the second chaaryaari, which comprised the sons and nephews of the first. And the treaties continued. Starting with Lord Minto, in August 1809, then two treaties during the governorship of Lord William Cavendish Bentinck in 1832 and 1834, through the agency of Sir Henry Pottinger. It was clearly stated in these treaties that the friendly feelings of the English Government towards Sindh would remain unaltered from generation to generation 'till the Day of Resurrection', and that the English Government would never covet one foot of the territory belonging to the Mirs of Sindh.

Enter Outram and Napier

In 1838, a new agreement was signed between the British and the Mirs, which was not at all in the interest of Sindh. A short while later, the British came out with yet another treaty comprising of twenty-three articles. Eastwick, accompanied by Captain James Outram, who had arrived in Sindh to replace Colonel Henry Pottinger, met the Mirs. They carried with them the draft of the new treaty of twenty-three articles to the Mirs. Nur Mohammad, most exasperated, produced a box full of papers and asked:

> "What is to become of all these? Since the day that Sindh has been connected with the British there has always been something new: your government is never satisfied, we are anxious for your friendship but we cannot be continually persecuted. We have given a road to your troops through our territories and now you wish to remain. This the Baloochis

> will never suffer...We have failed in nothing; we have furnished camels, boats, grains; we have distressed ourselves to supply your wants..."
>
> *Correspondence Relative to Sind: Eastwick to Pottinger, Jan 26, 1839*

The Talpur Mirs ruled successfully over an area of more than 100,000 square kilometres for a period of just sixty years, and were systematically vanquished by British intrigues and conspiracies. The most villainous of them, who made the final move which destroyed the Mirs, was Charles Napier, and he is said to have arrived in Sindh with instructions not to extend territory, which, as history shows us, he coolly ignored, focussing instead on the opportunities he observed. He wrote to Ellenborough: "Shikarpur contains many rich banking houses ... The money market is, generally speaking, the best political barometer."

When Napier came to Sindh, he was sixty. From what I have read, he hadn't had much success in his career. He had had a hard time supporting his daughters and was often in straitened circumstances. The Sindh posting

BATTLE OF MIANI
FROM *DRY LEAVES FROM YOUNG EGYPT* BY EDWARD EASTWICK (1849)

Sir Charles Napier c1860
From *Kurrachee* by Alexander Baillie

had been wangled for him through the influence of his older brother William, and he was determined to make the most of it and make his dreams come true before he became too old to fulfil them! However, he was unfamiliar with Sindh, had no knowledge of any Indian language or of the ways of the Mirs. To fulfil his dream of being recognized as an 'Alexander', a world conqueror, he provoked the Mirs with his authoritarian and overbearing ways. He confiscated their possessions on petty grounds. He accused them of forging documents, and of being disloyal to the Crown, particularly with reference to the First Afghan War which had ended as a major disaster for the British. He continued his provocation with unreasonable demands, and he rode roughshod over every situation.

The Mirs did not trust Napier, and sensed that he intended to wolfishly devour them even if they met all his demands. Outram understood the emotions of the Mirs and their resentment against Napier's harassment. He would have preferred to stand by the treaties which assured the Mirs of eternal friendship and respect for their territorial rights. In spite of Outram's repeated pleas of caution to Napier that the Mirs were not guilty of any breach of word, Napier fronted a brutal attack.

The Balochis fought bravely, and their numbers were large. On 17 February 1843, a historic clash took place at Miani. Sher Muhammad of Mirpur tried to rally forces, but could not match British firepower and he too was defeated at Dabbo on 24 March. Now nothing stood between Napier and his goal of annexing Sindh to the British Empire.

SETH NAOMAL HOTCHAND C1860
FROM *KURRACHEE* BY ALEXANDER BAILLIE

Some historians have criticized the role of Sindhi Hindu merchants, particularly of one Seth Naomal, whom they hold responsible for nurturing the seed of defection among some of the Balochi tribes. He has been labelled a 'traitor', having been awarded the Companion of the Most Exalted Order of Staff of Indian Empire (CIE) by the British after the annexation. Other historians argue that Naomal, an enormously wealthy zamindar and a businessman with innumerable contacts, dealt with the British only to enhance his own trade prospects.

And so, to end, my Management Studies course now has a fourth possible title derived from this last episode in the conquest of Sindh by the British, namely, 'How to Win by Deceit and Dishonesty'. Surely a hot seller at any Indian or international university!

4. A well-named street near my Calcutta home

After Caesar's succinct, "Veni, vidi, vici" – I came, I saw, I conquered – Napier's fictional, "Peccavi" – I have sinned – is considered to be the most laconic. I think fondly of the word 'laconic', especially when I listen to the endless speeches of most of our politicians. How I wish I lived in Laconia, the place in ancient Greece, where rulers gave the briefest of speeches!

Charles Napier, one of our British colonizers who flaunted extraordinary facial hair, certainly sinned. He wrote in his diary: "We have no right to seize Sindh, yet we shall do so, and a very advantageous, humane and useful piece of rascality it will be."

Outram had spent time in Sindh and was trusted by the Mirs. He tried to influence Napier, and he expressed himself clearly in a letter to him as he felt all the troubles in Sindh were the fault of the British. He wrote:

> It grieves me to say that my heart and the judgement God has given me, unite in condemning the measures we are carrying out ... as most tyrannical, positive robbery ...

Napier righteously wrote back: "If we are unjust in being here at all, at least let the people and ourselves draw from that injustice the benefit of civilization. This is my view, and I really think the Ameers' interests form a very minute ingredient in the business ..."

Napier ignored all civil rights. If there had been a treatise on the basic rights of individuals in the legal system of the time, he would have been convicted. The Mirs were dragged to prison where they languished till death proved a saviour[1]. The princesses and ladies of the court were dragged from their apartments, robbed of their jewels and thrown into prison without food or water. Napier himself, after attending the installation of the Union Jack, issued orders to loot the Talpur jewels and the utensils made of gold and silver and other valuable treasures.

According to the records I have read, Sir Charles Napier was appointed Governor of Sindh after he annexed it, with emoluments of Rs8000 per month, a tidy sum for the time. The point that interested me most, however, more than Napier's monthly salary or even the Machiavellian tactics adopted by him and Ellenborough, was the name of Sir James Outram. It was a name I recognized, having grown up in Calcutta in the 1950s. In this erstwhile capital of the British Empire, I was more familiar with European History and with the names of British military officers and their brave exploits than with my own Indian History. We lived at Short Street; our school Loreto House was at Middleton Row. Wellesley Street was the street where we went to buy all our schoolbooks. Then there was Harrington Street, Lansdowne Road, Brabourne Road, Bentinck Street, Wellington Square, and others. And there was Outram Street. You could get acquainted with British History by simply taking a guided trip through the city.

Indian governments have changed the names of several cities in an attempt to reclaim them from the colonizers. Pondicherry became Puducherry; Madras became Chennai; Bangalore became Bengaluru, and so forth. Calcutta is now Kolkata.

---

1 *Talpurs in Sindh* by Dr Mumtaz Hussain Pathan (Karachi Endowment Fund Trust) reviewed and Quoted in *Dawn*

Inside Calcutta

Within Calcutta, even street names and road names are changing rapidly. The Road Renaming Committee of the Kolkata Municipal Corporation is the hardest working committee in the world! Seventeen of its streets were recently re-named by Chief Minister Mamta Banerjee. There is even a 23-page booklet published by the KMC which lists the new names of roads, streets, ghats and setus – bridges – which have been re-named.

As a devoted citizen of Calcutta who would cast a vote for Calcutta and its loveable people against Bombay any day, I really value its taxi drivers and friendly bus conductors who helpfully hold on to the old names and never get confused! There is nobody as chivalrous as a Calcutta bus driver or conductor. They stop the bus gallantly even mid-road if a lady wishes to get off or on. If it was not for them, several people in Calcutta may have committed suicide by jumping from the nearest setu after being unable to locate an address. I'm not sure I'd ever want to tell a taxi driver to take me to Tara Pada Santrakela Sarani!

However, one little beacon remains: the name of Outram Street has not been changed. I asked some of my more erudite friends in Calcutta the reason for KMC sparing this beautiful, secluded little street which has so many historic landmarks. One of them, a senior citizen from an old bhadralok Calcutta family, told me philosophically that it would entail too much trouble for the KMC.

"Why?" I asked, "KMC has done yeoman service in re-naming most of Calcutta and in addition even brought out a booklet of 23 microscopically-printed pages, cataloguing the new names. And why did they ignore our poor Outram Street?" I asked peevishly, feeling personally affronted because my family lives just three-and-a-half minutes away from Outram Street. A logical explanation was provided forthwith: "It is too much hard work to change the name of Outram Street because then the names of many major landmarks of the city will also have to be changed."

This set me thinking: which were these landmarks? The first that promptly came to my mind was the Outram Club at No 3, Outram Street. It is a comfortable, homely old club with a variety of cuisines. Colonel Outram, who was generous with donating books and money may even have donated something to this club. A lot of work is involved in attempting to change the name of a historic club and the club trustees may never agree.

Then there is the Carmelite Convent at No 4, Outram Street. For the past eighty years, this colonial-style bungalow has served as the residence of the Carmelite nuns. International visitors come to seek solace from these revered sisters, who never come out but speak from behind a screen. I too visit the Carmelite nuns on every visit to Calcutta and speak to them through the screen and feel greatly comforted. The adjacent church here is another grand monument. Changing the name of the street would alter its cultural heritage, from which so many continue to derive spiritual succour and comfort.

OUTRAM CLUB, PARK STREET AREA, KOLKATA
IMAGE COURTESY ANITA SAMIR MUKHERJEE

Next comes Outram Ghat, where we went every year to see the beautiful idols being immersed during the Durga Puja festival. In the breezy summer months, we had evening picnics there with loads of food and rounded off dinner with a chocolate-covered ice-cream stick from the ice-cream cart-wallah. And if a boatman was around, a cruise down the river in the traditional wooden boat was a treat.

And finally, we have our famous Outram Statue which originally stood in the Maidan. As youngsters we sat under its shadow and chatted. Now though it has changed location to within the Victoria Memorial, it still brings back sweet memories!

James Outram

After this bout of nostalgia, I began to ponder why Lieutenant Colonel James Outram should hold such an important place in the hearts of our people. All I knew was that he had served in several cities of India – not just Calcutta but also Lucknow and Hyderabad (Sindh). He had been felicitated by Oxford University on his return to England. And then I came across more details which showed that James Outram does deserve this pride of place in the hearts of the people of India. And particularly in the hearts of the people of Sindh, for his relentless single-handed fight for the rights of the Mirs against the powers-that-be in England, even after his retirement from service.

Before the arrival of Napier in Sindh, Outram had been in charge of negotiations between the British and the Mirs. He had been lenient, honest, and understanding towards them, which they appreciated greatly. With the arrival of Napier everything changed. For Napier was authoritarian, wanted full control and most of all, he longed for military campaigns and victories that would make him famous. This created a major rift between the two men which continued for years, and was carried over to Home territory as well – 'Home' being the euphemism by which colonials spoke of their faraway homeland, ruling on its behalf from distant shores.

Outram was humane and more interested in the welfare of people than in dominating them. He belonged to that group of high-minded and selfless British servants whose life was not only devoted to the service of the Crown but also to the civilized and considerate treatment of all.

When he returned to England in May 1843, his mind was tortured with the unfortunate condition of the Mirs and the great controversy on the annexation of Sindh, and the differences of opinion between Napier and himself. He made representations on behalf of the Mirs, and this proved a long and costly affair. For years the uncongenial paper warfare dragged on, and was the source of much pain and unhappiness to him.

Before the annexation, Napier had praised Outram and proudly bestowed on him the title of 'Bayard of India'. But the Sindh chapter and Outram's support of the Mirs made Napier lose much of the glory he felt he had achieved. He was criticized by liberal humanists not only in England but also by high-ranking British civilians in India and in later years would be ranked alongside the infamous General Dyer, who ordered the shooting of innocent people in the Jalianwala Bagh at Amritsar in 1919. Sir William, the brother who had arranged for Sir Charles's posting, came out staunchly in support. But even this did not help Charles Napier to retain his sheen or glory!

Outram was presented by the High Command with a sword of honour, three hundred guineas, and a costly piece of plate, as a token of the high esteem he was held

Sir James Outram

in by his peers. He was promoted to the rank of Lieutenant Colonel. I have read that he distributed his monetary rewards among charitable institutions in India. He resigned his seat in the Council of the Viceroy, and after a public felicitation in Calcutta, left India.

I cannot possibly end here! A few days ago, I received a call from my brother Ajit in Calcutta with whom I had discussed the renaming of Outram Street.

He was in a philosophical mood and said: "You know, since we talked about it, I discussed the renaming of Outram Street with my friend who is close to senior KMC officials. And he told me that the renaming of several small streets is definitely in the pipeline, once people have got used to the seventeen street names that have been changed recently."

Not MY Outram Street!" I shrieked. And tried to explain to Ajit the nobility of a person about whom the Bombay Service proudly said, "A fox is a fool and a lion a coward compared with James Outram."

And then came Ajit's memorable parting shot: "I do hope they name it after Mamta Didi! Don't you?"

I banged the phone down. My head was spinning. I immediately ordered a large dab – coconut – from the vendor downstairs. I didn't know whose head I should bash! Mine or my brother's. It seems that the next time I'm in Kolkata I may not be able to locate Outram Street. Instead, I may have to jump down some setu! Or latch onto some bold, chivalrous bus conductor's arm!

5. If you can't go to Sindh
... just fly to Egypt

One of the first books recommended to me when I showed interest in the study of Sindh was *Dry leaves from young Egypt*. On hearing the title, I dismissed it, assuming it to be about the flora and fauna of Egypt. But later, when it was twice recommended by friends who insisted it would add to my knowledge of Sindh, I looked around and found it sitting on my own bookshelf at home. And once I started reading it, I found it such a thrilling tale of adventurous travel, interwoven with so much fascinating detail, that I just could not put it down!

The author, Edward Backhouse Eastwick, was a young British officer who joined the Bombay infantry in 1836. Owing to his talent for languages, he was given a political posting. Among his many works is a Sindhi Grammar. Besides colourful and charming descriptions of the author's experiences in Sindh, *Dry leaves from young Egypt* is an expose of the shameless way in which the British treated the Talpur Mirs. It was subsequently published under the title *A Glance at Sind Before Napier*. The British were new to Sindh and, in this book, Eastwick likened it to Egypt, a place they were more familiar with.

As I continued my research, I found that other scholars and critics had also noted the similarity between Sindh and Egypt. Among these were the archaeologist Henry Cousens, and the British Orientalist and diplomat H T Lambrick. Both compare the two ancient lands and note their similarities. These observations filled me with the thought, "Well, if I can't visit my homeland Sindh, maybe I should just go to Egypt!"

The comparison between the two countries is interesting:

- Both countries have the same three tracts: hills, alluvial plain and sandy desert.
- The vegetation in both countries is characteristic of a dry and arid climate.
- The Nile and the Indus in both countries flood in a way that creates abundant and rich, finely-grained, alluvial soil.
- The seasons are much alike in both countries, hot and cold, without the gradations of spring and autumn.
- In both places there is absence of rain except in the delta areas, and the deltas of both rivers are known for their copious quantities of dew.
- Though in its upper plain, the Indus has several tributaries, in its lower plain it is like the Nile in having only a few tributaries.
- Another wonderful similarity between both rivers is that they are given a spiritual significance and the people worship their rivers and celebrate their inundation.
- Both Sindh and Egypt have salty sands. In Egypt, mummies were preserved by embalming corpses in a sand which was rich in salt and nitrogen. Sindh, too, is rich in salt. At the Rann of Kachchh, one of the largest salt deserts in the world, one is literally walking on silvery salty sand!
- During the First World War, the British army created the Egyptian Camel Transport Corps which consisted of a group of Egyptian camels. Our camels of Sindh too were used in the Imperial Service Corps.

The Bikaner Camel Corps or Ganga Risala, formed by Maharaja Ganga Singh (1887-1943), fought in China, Somaliland, Egypt and the Middle East as part of the British Army in India. It is now part of the Indian Army's Border Security Force. As part of the Border Security Force they maintain long vigils on their camels in the extreme heat of the border region of the Thar desert.

The books by British officials in Sindh were quick to assert

Photograph of a sowar (rider) of the Bikaner Camel Corps on his mount, Bikaner, Rajasthan, taken by an unknown photographer during Viceroy Lord Elgin's 'Autumn Tour 1896'

one major difference: they believed that the civilization of Egypt was much older than the civilization of Sindh. Just a few decades after these books were written, they themselves stumbled upon the ruins of the Indus Valley Civilization which of course was found to be much older than the Egyptian. This establishes yet another similarity – the fascinating archeological ruins of ancient civilizations that both Egypt and Sindh host.

One of Eastwick's amusing characters is Andrew Ross Bell, a civilian from the British administration of Bengal, whose official designation was 'Political Agent of Sindh and Balochistan'. His behaviour, Eastwick observes, was that of a de facto dictator. Eastwick, a conscientious twenty-five-year-old, was summoned by this 'great' man, and expected to receive instruction on general political policy. Instead, he was arrogantly ordered to ensure that Bell's household was regularly supplied with fresh green peas. Eastwick continues, "Fourteen thousand bottles of beer annually poured forth their foaming contents at his board." When he travelled, "several hundred camels conveyed vast supplies of beer, wine and stores of all descriptions ... yet there remained then still in store at the Agency, among other items, twelve hundred dozens of beer, and one hundred and twenty dozens of champagne." It seems likely that many Englishmen posted in India, referred to by anti-Imperialists as 'the scum of England' must have lived as Andrew Ross Bell did!

In the 1843 issue of *The Journal of the Royal Asiatic Society of Great Britain*, John W Parker, who had visited both Egypt and Sindh, wrote:

> It can hardly fail to strike the traveller that there is a great similarity in these two rivers, between the ports by which both are accessible from the sea: Karachee is to the Indus what Alexandria is

> to the Nile and in our (British) hands ... the result of (our) good government, shall hereafter bring about such a revolution in that state of the country watered by the Indus, as to make Karachee the Alexandria of the Indian Ocean.

The potential of Karachi's harbour had already been realized by the British who were camping in Karachi when these lines were written. And soon, under Napier, it became the capital of Sindh.

My grandmother often told me that "our Sindhu nadi" regularly changed its course, which I found hard to believe. After all, in my school map book, the rivers ran in definite fixed lines! Only countries changed boundaries when they were conquered by other countries, or when larger counties usurped land from them.

Now I understood that both rivers – the Nile and the Indus – have changed course as long-lived old rivers historically do change course. But the difference is that the Indus has been more whimsical and changeable – just like its Sindhi people! And, like us, unmindful of our history, it has wiped out so much of our past. Today it is often difficult to identify the location of our ancient cities. The movement of the Nile, on the other hand, has been slow, often blocked by rocks in the earth's deep surface.

Behrano Sahib

Whenever my father was planning to travel, my grandmother would give him *akho* to put in the water. After I married and my husband travelled out of the city on business, I saw that his mother too would give him *akho* to appease the water gods so that he would have a safe journey. *Akho*, a mixture of a little rice mixed with sugar and flour, is offered to a body of water (the sea, a lake, a river, or pond), usually on a full moon day.

One of our Sindhi traditions is to celebrate an event by taking out a Behrano in a procession. This cult started with the periodic flooding of the holy river, which generally commenced by the end of March and continued through May, peaking in August. The Behrano evolved as an offering and thanksgiving to the water god.

The Behrano Sahib is a decorated **thaal** – large plate – on which an idol of Jhulelal is placed. The **thaal** is decorated with fruits and flowers, with diyas lit around it. A small **kŭnrï** – earthen pot – of water is kept on the **thaal** as well. Devotees cover their heads and carry the Behrano Sahib, dancing and singing devotional songs, down to the water. The immersion is followed by distribution of **tahïrï** – sweet rice – prasad.

As the source of sustenance and occasional destruction, the Nile, too, influenced religion, shaping the conditions in which ancient Egyptians developed their religious rites. According to Egyptian mythology, the god Osiris was drowned in the Nile. The annual inundation was regarded as water emanating from his body. Water had life-giving virtues, it gave vitality to the earth, and this led to the emergence of plant life, and celebrations ensued.

People living along the Nile encountered hippopotamuses, and one of their goddesses Taweret, took the form of a hippopotamus. With the Sindhis, the earliest representation of the Indus god was made in the form of a human deity sitting on a fish floating on water – Jhulelal to the Hindus; Khwaja Khizr to the Muslims.

With travel restrictions to Pakistan so tight, I expect a long wait for the documentation to come through before I can kiss the soil of my beloved lost homeland! Meanwhile – why not visit Egypt! I think I might just do that.

6. Chikni Chachi from Tando Adam

The town of Tando Adam in Sindh has fond memories for me – even though I have never been there and, sadly, never will. It is where my beloved aunt Urmila Chachi grew up. Let me tell you an interesting story regarding her engagement.

Sketch of an elderly Sindhi lady who resembles my Nani. Seen wearing a traditional nose ornament, the natha. Worn by married women, the natha usually had a large oval ruby set with pearls, and a gold pin that was inserted in the hole pierced in the nose. The heavy natha was supported by a horse's hair which was woven into the woman's plait to help support it.
Image by Bhagwan Khilnani (first appeared in *Aseen Sindhi* magazine Aug-Sep 1997)

My Nani, my mother's mother, Tehemal bai Makhijani, had four daughters, and my Dadi, my father's mother Vanat bai Nain, had four sons.

Nani's eldest daughter married Dadi's first-born son. Since the families knew each other and were happy with the first alliance, Nani's second daughter, Parvati, was given in marriage to Dadi's second son, Lokumal. Parvati was fifteen; Lokumal was twenty-four. In time, they would be my parents.

In those days, family background was considered important, and 'love' had not yet been discovered! Psychologists and psychiatrists and the definition of love's various facets and degrees lay in the future, as did the lucrative profession of marriage counselling. It was well known that when elders decided a match, a couple would grow together and breed, and would most likely come to know and respect each other too. Passion was never discussed, even if it crept secretly into a marriage (or outside it). The guiding principle in marriage was stability, and parents made every effort to instill the corresponding values in their sons and daughters. If a man had an affair or a lover, the family stayed silent, hoping that the straying husband would come to his senses, prioritize the warmth and comfort of his own family, and discontinue his philandering. Women in Sindhi families were relatively better treated than those in neighbouring provinces where the practice of sati, in which a woman is expected to consign herself to her husband's funeral pyre, was prevalent.

Both my parents came from refined Sahiti families which were socially on par. But when it came to the question of Dadi's son number three, Lachhmandas, marrying Nani's daughter number three, Dadi Vanat bai blew a fuse and raised her hands in strong opposition: "Two girls from the same family are married to my two sons. Are there no other Sahiti girls in the whole of Sindh?" she inquired belligerently. (And who could blame her? Who would want three sisters ganging up against their mother-in-law under the leadership of daughter-in-law number one?)

So Nain son number three was not given in marriage to Makhijani daughter number three.

In the meantime, a friend from the Manghnani family suggested Urmila, a girl from a good Bhaiband family. And so it was that the marriage of son number three took place in Bombay, in post-Partition India in 1950, and Urmila Chachi became a part of our family. And when Makhijani daughter number four married a Nain cousin, Dadi's loud mutters of disapproval were audible to all.

Urmila Chachi was from a Sindhworki Bhaiband family of Tando Adam, and a different kind of breeze began to flow into our simple conservative Sahiti family. Urmila Chachi was outgoing, extremely friendly, came from a large family, and was used to doing just as she pleased.

In contrast, my mother and her elder sister were both simple in dress, simple in their cooking, and single-mindedly intent on saving every pie so that they could give their children the best professional education. These were pre-Partition girls of a certain mould. But Urmila Chachi, who married in 1950, good-naturedly ignored the austerity

The author's mother (standing left) and two aunts; Urmila Chachi, her head covered and touching shoulders with Dadi Vanat Bai; the author as a child, with thick plaits; her sister Mira. Touching Mira's shoulder is their masi-chachi Mrs J L Nain (wife of Justice JL Nain)
Image courtesy Madan Nain

of the Sahiti family she had married into. She craved for diamonds, more gold jewellery, fashionable clothes, and gourmet food – and these were certainly qualities that endeared us youngsters to her!

When Urmila Chachi and Uncle Lachhman made their home in Calcutta, we enjoyed lavish meals of *keema ka naan, chakla velan besan bhaji, sayal phulka,* and *sanha pakoda*. Even her *saee bhaji* had a touch of its own as she would put in all the vegetables along with the onions, garlic and ginger, and we loved it. It was different from our Sahiti *saee bhaji*, which was prepared with just greens! *Saee bhaji* is of course a staple food in a Sindhi household, apart from being the barometer to judge good cooking. Like dhansak is for the Parsis and shorsher machh (or aloo poshto) is for the Bengalis, *saee bhaji* is the Sindhi's basic comfort food. Every bride must know how to make it! It was the one dish my mother insisted I learn to prepare, the week before my marriage.

And Urmila Chachi loved serving us mouth-watering sweet dishes. At my parents' Sahiti home in those days when guests visited for a meal, a colourful shivering jelly was the staple dessert – easy to make and easy to serve. Milk was scarce. The Amul cooperative and India's illustrious 'milkman', Dr Kurien Verghese, were still in the future. So we were never sure if there would be enough milk for custard or any other sweet dish! But Urmila Chachi somehow always managed to churn out a mouth-watering three-tiered delicacy: jelly, china grass and custard crowned with a variety of colourful fruits. Her ice cream with falooda was something to die for and her khorak, laden with all the dry fruits that the world had to offer, was a dream!

Bhau Murijmal

When Urmila Chachi's Sindhworki brother, Bhau Murijmal Manghnani, landed in Bombay from Dubai and travelled to Calcutta to meet his sister, he invariably came laden with two bottles of Black Label whisky for my father, and a large box of chocolates.

My father rarely indulged in a drink but when the Black Label came my dadi would say, "Loku, since the bottle is out, give me a *chuṭki* too. It is good for my aches and pains." And my father and dadi would sit down and enjoy a liberal swig together. There is a lot to be learnt from the Bhaiband hospitality and generosity.

One of my memories is of Urmila Chachi's old father, Dada Jiwatram. He lived in Bombay, and would always come to see my father off at the railway station when my father was travelling back from Bombay to Calcutta, with a tiffin box in one hand and innumerable goodies in the other, for the two-night train journey.

Savitri and Jiwatram Manghnani
image courtesy Rachna Manghnani, their daughter-in-law

The Sindhworkis had been trading in ports around the world for nearly a hundred years before Partition took place, and had created a solid base for many displaced Sindhis to venture into foreign lands for trade, and Bhau Murijmal had been one of those who did so.

His sister was our family's daughter-in-law, and this gave us a special status – we were his respected ***saïns*** – in-laws! He would always greet my father by bending down and touching his feet. The Bhaibands are very respectful to elders. There is much diving down and touching of feet to seek blessings.

The Dignified Bhaiband Dive

It must be noted at this point that the dive in the Bhaiband community is different from the dive practiced in Calcutta where I grew up. While performing the Bengali dive, the feet of the elders must be touched gently with the tips of the fingers by bending low from the waist down (even if you suffer from back problems!) But among the Bhaibands, you must bend delicately down just up to the knee-level of the elder one. Just a gentle, elegant bend.

An elderly uncle gave me a demo when he saw me bending clumsily deep down to touch feet with my saree pallu flying immodestly in all directions. He admonished: "There is no need to dive right down and touch toes. Such a dive may spoil your hairdo or undo your saree-pleats, or worse still, rip apart the top hook of your tightly-fitted choli, leaving the young men to throng around, eager for more!"

And the Bhaibands do look at their women, their own wives and other men's wives! They like their women to look good and display their clothes and jewellery. This gives the husbands the advantage of looking prosperous. If the wife looks good, the husband must be affluent. Good to do business with!

The information about the Bhaiband dive from the elderly uncle was a relief to me for I had found myself performing innumerable dives as a new bride and was fearful of the resultant impact on my vertebral column. My parents had admonished me, "Dive! Dive immediately when you behold an elder approaching. It is a strict custom in the Bhaiband community, and they expect it of you. Traditions have to be followed. Otherwise they will think our highly-educated Sahiti community slips short of good manners. And you will be considered arrogant and **matho firyal** – head in the air – because of your 'high' education!" I was quite horrified to see even my mother diving down to my mother-in-law. My mother was about ten years younger than my mother-in-law, but I suspect that she would have done the dive even if she had been the older one.

I did notice that the Bhaiband community as a whole is more open and demonstrative, while we Sahiti people are more quiet and reserved. My father and his Sahiti relatives would never discuss financial deals, profits or business matters with anyone – but Bhaibands are ostentatiously open and make no secret of their wealth or business profits. (Sometimes they are rudely called "showy and vulgar" by those who envy them!)

And language! I had heard only gentle words in my Sahiti home. But after my marriage in the Bhaiband household, the use of choice abuses, such as **mua, gareeviya, chariya** were quite common – and **behenchod, sallaa, kanyar kameena, chutiya** all of which I shall decline from translating for you, were even commoner! When I reprimanded my husband once about his over-colourful vocabulary and his generous use of every lewd word in the Sindhi dictionary, he smiled and said, "My love, we Bhaibands use these swear words most affectionately. We even give *bŭjo* and *bhoondo* – hand gestures which convey contempt – lovingly! But we don't mean to curse anybody. I love my Sindhi language and I know all aspects of it well. But, as you know, I also love your 'propah' Queen's English!"

Whether it is the Bhaiband businessman of Bombay or the Bhaiband Sindhworki who sails the seven seas, there is some similarity in their behaviour and habits. They are loving, generous, open, and easygoing. And philanthropic. And ready to help. Many of the hospitals and charitable institutions in Bombay have been initiated by Sindhi Bhaibands and Sindhworkis.

***

Tando Adam, I have realized of late, the lost hometown of my Urmila Chachi, in our imagination a charming and delightful place to yearn nostalgically for, is today the rather nondescript fifty-seventh largest city of Pakistan, with a population of 153,000. North-east of Hyderabad, south-west of Sanghar, it lies significantly to the south-east of Nawabshah and more towards Sehwan. It is a good bit inland from our magnificent Sindhu.

Ah, each of these names creates a ripple of nostalgia in me – nostalgia for these places so replete with sweet, fresh memories! Places I have never seen and, sadly, never will. And yet, I do feel justified in ending this with a tribute to my Urmila Chachi's ever-buoyant and big-hearted community:

> Go East or West,
> Bhaibands are the best!

7. Our Rohri-Sukkur heritage

Growing up in Calcutta, I had never heard of Sadh Belo. But no sooner had I re-located to Bombay after my marriage than Sadh Belo became an important part of my life. A month after my marriage came the Diwali week, and my family suggested we go to Mahalaxmi Mandir and Sadh Belo. A couple of days later, on pooran-masi (full moon), we made another trip to make an offering. The visit on Cheti Chand, the Sindhi New Year, was always compulsory. Later, a cousin's two-year-old baby boy was having his *mŭndan* ceremony (ritual shaving of a baby's first hair) and we had to go to bless the child. There were regular occasions on which the family made it mandatory that we should go. I enjoyed these visits to Sadh Belo – except the one on Cheti Chand, when it was always overcrowded.

At first I felt confused: was Mahalaxmi Temple another name for Sadh Belo? The two seemed synonymous as the family always announced, "Today we will go to Mahalaxmi!"

It was later that I realized that the whole complex is referred to as Mahalaxmi Mandir but the actual Mahalakshmi Mandir is a few yards uphill and we didn't go there because the senior members of the family found the climb difficult. So one morning I decided to make a trip on my own. And even ended up having a good breakfast there! Here are the directions.

If you enter by the Shiva Temple Gate (easily identifiable because there is a kabutar-khana on the left and you can feed the pigeons if you want), you will be able to visit a trio of temples to Lord Shiva opposite the kabutar-khana. A few steps forward and you see the beautiful and peaceful Sadh Belo dedicated to Lord Krishna. It has a large hall, and the walls are decorated with paintings depicting episodes from the life of Lord Krishna. This was the sanctum we visited most often. But if you proceed further, there is a pathway lined with flower-sellers and hawkers selling puja items. And another line of food stalls which cannot be ignored, particularly the moong-dal bhajiya seller. Keep this in mind for the return journey! If you climb further up the hill, you will arrive at the beautiful main Mahalakshmi Mandir, ringed by the Arabian Sea on three sides, a view that makes the climb well worthwhile.

IRB and I made a special visit to Sadh Belo on Vandana's first birthday to seek the blessings of the family Maharaj. After chanting a blessing for our little girl, the Maharaj tied a black thread on her wrist, to ward off the evil eye.

That evening we visited the home of my uncle (the late Justice J L Nain) in Bandra. As a child, I had spent summer holidays with them and was close to Raju, their daughter-in-law, who was from a Rohri family. When Raju saw the black thread on Vandana's wrist, she was thrilled, and asked where we had got it. I told her about our Sadh Belo trip, and was surprised when her old nostalgic memories poured forth spontaneously:

> I visited Sadh Belo in Rohri quite a number of times. I was seven or eight years old when Partition took place. Lots of our families used to have the **mŭndan** ceremony in Sadh Belo on the banks of the Sindhu River. It used to be such fun as we had to travel by boat. Sadh Belo stood between Rohri and Sukkur on a tear-shaped island. A visit there was a full-day picnic for us children. They also had langar there all day, and we enjoyed that the most!

As she looked out of her window recalling memories from the past, I could see her eyes moisten. Her father had passed away in 1947, just a few months before Partition, after suffering a massive stroke, when he was just thirty-nine. Her young mother hardly had the time to mourn, as she had to bear the immense burden of fleeing from Rohri with five small children and her aged mother.

But Raju, as brave as her mother and possessing that Sindhi never-say-die gene, continued to recount her bagful of nostalgic memories:

> While sitting in Sadh Belo, we could see Lansdowne Bridge and its elegant cantilevers. It was built to connect our twin towns of Rohri and Sukkur, and we felt so proud of it. Do you know, it had no pillars – it was the eighth wonder of the world! On the other side we caught glimpses of Zinda Pir Khwaja Khizr.
>
> We loved to see movies, and there were no cinema houses in Rohri so we had to visit Sukkur where all the latest movies were screened. I remember two of the movies we saw there, *Ratan* and *Dasi*. My father also had to go to the Imperial Bank for his hundi and banking matters, and that was also in Sukkur. So we would walk there, across the footbridge, quite often."

Sadh Belo

I later read that Sadh Belo, the hermitage of monks, is situated on a vast complex spread across two connected islands in the middle of the Sindhu – Sadh Belo and Deen Belo. It was established in 1823 by Baba Bankhandi, a monk of the Udasipanth, the sect founded by Baba Sri Chand, the eldest son of Guru Nanak.

Sadh Belo was an important Udasi shrine and a site of

DARBAR OF BABA BANKHANDI AT SADH BELO
IMAGE COURTESY ZULFIQAR ALI KALHORO

pilgrimage for Hindus and Sikhs, but by the end of the 19th century, the power and influence of the Udasi sect had begun to decline. Sadh Belo, located as it was in our liberal Sindh, which was hospitable soil to every sect, continued to thrive. Baba Bankhandi's grand darbar hall had been built by 1889. Marble was imported from Jaipur and intricate carvings adorn some of the buildings of Sadh Belo. It also had a large library, a residential establishment for monks, and the samadhis of its main priests. New temples and shrines continued to be built, dedicated to a range of holy figures including Annapurna, Hanuman, Ganesh, Shiva, the Bhagwad Gita and the Guru Granth Sahib.

Sadh Belo was attended by Muslims as well. After Partition, with the campaign to rid Sindh of its Hindus, even the head priest of Sadh Belo was evacuated to Bombay. Today I believe this large heritage complex, one of the largest surviving temples in Pakistan, is in the custody of Pakistan's

Evacuee Property Trust Board.

"I suppose now Sadh Belo must be quite deserted," I said to Raju.

"Yes, I heard from a relative who was able to visit in the days when it was possible to get a visa, that there is not much maintenance now. The kitchens which were once fragrant with the langar food are now deserted. Even the boats between Rohri and Sukkur which would take us to Sadh Belo ply infrequently."

"I have been told," I said, "even Zulfikar Bhutto and his mother used to come to Sadh Belo in those days. Did you see them there?"

"Yes, they used to come. I would not have recognized them. But my mother used to say that she saw Bhutto's mother there quite often, and sometimes her son came too."

I remember reading that Zulfiqar Ali Bhutto's mother was Hindu. According to KR Malkani[1] her name was Lakhan bai before she became Khurshid. And Bhagwan Gidwani wrote in *Return of the Aryans*:

> In my student days, at Sadhbela (a famous Hindu temple) at Sukkur in Sindh, I saw Zulfiqar Ali Bhutto, who was known to us as Zulfie then. He was at a Langar, the community meal of Sadhbela, and I also saw him taking away a little halwa, which was served with the meal. He could not have been there just for the free meal, for he was always flush with money. Maybe he was there to render thanks for a wish fulfilled, or to seek blessings for a wish for the future. I don't know. I sat with him and exchanged greetings, for like many of us, I had enjoyed the hospitality of his household at Larkana, but certainly did not ask him why he

1 *The Sindh Story* by KR Malkani (1984) p127

> was at Sadhbela. Recently, a South Indian friend questioned me, "How come no one asked Bhutto, why he was there?"
>
> Only a non-Sindhi would ask such a question. For us, it was not too uncommon in Sindh to see Hindus in dargahs and Muslims at Hindu holy places.... Sindhi Muslims accepted our ancient heritage of Mooan jo Daro as their own. When Muslims from India poured into Sindh, bent on loot and massacre, it was Sindhi Muslims who protected Hindus.

A SANCTUM WHERE WISHES ARE GRANTED

On another occasion I asked a friend who was also from Rohri if he had ever visited Satiyan jo Asthan, which I had read about, a temple located on the left bank of River Indus in Rohri right next to Sukkur.

He laughed.

"What's the matter?" I asked peevishly. "It's not a funny question! I'm writing a book on Sindh."

"My dear," he said, "Men are not allowed to enter there."

"Why?" I asked, surprised, though quite pleased at the idea. Good to have a place where men are prohibited. After all the havoc of women having to use force to enter the Sabarimala Temple in Kerala. And women previously not being allowed into the Lord Kartikeya Temple in Pushkar, the Patbausi Satra temple in Assam, and so many others.

"Well I don't know too much history," he replied, "but from what I've heard, the reason dates back to the time of Muhammad bin Qasim and Raja Dahirsen. When Bin Qasim defeated the Hindu king Raja Dahir, seven women fleeing to save themselves chose this hilly area as their abode. And when bin Qasim set his gaze on them, they prayed to God to save them and they were sucked into the earth as they knelt in prayer. This site has several graves, seven of which stand out because of their prominent and intricate carvings. They are supposedly the graves of those seven sisters."

Then he added, much amused, "When the day comes that we are allowed to travel to Pakistan, I will take you and you can pray for me to become a multi-millionaire. Your wish will surely come true."

"Yes, of course it will," I replied sarcastically, "That will be my only wish! Do you men pray for us women when you visit 'men only' temples?"

He just laughed and I had the last word when I muttered to myself, "Silly male."

I'm glad he didn't hear that. And I'm happy that when he reads my book, he will see a picture of Satiyan jo Asthan on its cover, even if he can never enter!

Sava lakha pir

Rohri was famous for the holy men attached to its tombs and mosques. It was seen as hallowed land, where these wandering mendicants proliferated to such an extent that there were more than a hundred and twenty-five thousand of them! And, if an article in *Dawn* newspaper is to be believed, these pirs continued to perform their miracles even long after their Hindu devotees had been chased away from their ancestral homeland. Entitled *The Saint Who saved Rohri, Sukkur and Lansdowne Bridge during 1965 War*, the reporter wrote that she was being driven across the Lansdowne Bridge and could see the twin cities of Sukkur and Rohri on either side of the river. Suddenly the driver pointed to a dilapidated structure and told her: "Khwaja Khizr saved us from destruction!"

She was not sure what he meant, and he elaborated: "During the India-Pakistan war, people noticed a green-robed man standing over the bridge and disabling the bombs. That is how Lansdowne Bridge and Rohri and Sukkur were saved."

Khwaja Khizr is revered by both Hindus and Muslims, as an incarnation of the holy River Indus. Only with one difference: *we* call him Udero Lal or Jhulelal or Zinda Pir and regard him as our 'Ishtadevta', our protector who took care of us when we were forced to flee, leaving our homeland for ever.

UNASSUMING BUT PROFICIENT

The best-known Sindhi communities are Amils, Bhaibands, Shikarpuris, Sahiti and a few others. Unfortunately, not much is known about the people of Rohri as they are by and large unassuming and modest. But they are amongst the most enlightened and educated of the communities of Sindh. Before Partition, the Bhaibands were extremely mobile, and travelled to wherever they saw business and trading opportunities. The Shikarpuris had set up their *pedhis* in several places in India and outside. And the Amils had their contacts in Bombay, as Sindh was part of Bombay Presidency under the British, until 1936. But for the people of the interior town of Rohri, though rich in culture and committed to education and hard work, it was a different story.

Colonial writers have mentioned the beautiful textiles produced in Rohri which were exported to many places. These were preserved as heirlooms and passed down from mother to daughter. What they appear to have avoided mentioning is that the area around Rohri-Sukkur was a hotbed of the Indian struggle from colonial rule.

One of its martyrs was the young patriot, Hemu Kalani. Born in 1923, he joined in the campaign for boycott of foreign goods, and at a young age began leading the revolutionary struggle during the 1942 Quit India movement. One day, news arrived that a train carrying British military personnel with arms and ammunition would be travelling from Quetta to Sukkur, both large army cantonment towns, to quell the protests. Hemu and two accomplices decided to protest by removing fish plates on the railway track and derailing the train. They were spotted and chased, and Hemu was captured while the others managed to escape. Hemu was offered a pardon if he would reveal the names of his accomplices. Despite all the intimidation and beating he was subject to, he remained resolutely silent right until he was led to the gallows. This was the spirit of a nineteen-year-old Sindhi patriot!

These are qualities that are not generally associated with Sindhis.

We are looked upon as a business community with global successes like the Jagtianis of the Landmark Group in the Middle East; the extraordinary Wadhwani brothers, Romesh and Sunil, with hugely successful IT companies in the US and magnificent philanthropic foundations in India; Chhabrias of Finolex; the Tolanis of Tolani Shipping and the prestigious Tolani Maritime Institute; the old five Bhaiband names Chellarams, Chainrais, Harilelas, Watumulls, Wassiamulls – and many, many more.

Somehow, it has been overlooked that we Sindhis have a very large population of remarkably successful professionals too. Many have risen to the top by sheer dint of hard work and that unconquerable will which defines the character of a Sindhi. The two whose work I will now tell you about were extraordinary individuals whom I have known and observed at close quarters. Both came to Bombay in the wake of Partition. They completed their education in Bombay and started as young professionals. One is DM Harish, who studied law, specializing in Income Tax law. The other is Manohar Keswani, who became a doctor. Both these remarkable men are remembered today for the institutions they initiated and nurtured, and for their philanthropy.

DM Harish

'Dada DM', as we affectionately called him, was from Rohri. He graduated from DJ Sind College in Karachi and then married Ratna Gurnani (Aunty Ratni to us) from Sukkur, just across the river. When Partition compelled them to flee leaving everything behind, they arrived in Bombay. Dada DM joined the Government Law College at Churchgate. A few years later, Aunty Ratni also joined the law college and on completion of her studies joined as a partner of the law firm M/s DM Harish and Co. Her elder sister, Saraswati Gurnani, was among the earliest Sindhi women to take up higher education, joining DJ Sind College in 1933-34. She became a teacher and was so highly regarded that she was hired to teach the children of Rajendra Prasad, India's first President, for which she visited Rashtrapati Bhavan every day. Dada DM's brother, Dr DM Dayal, became a well-known doctor; and his brother DM Ramesh took up real-estate development, with a grand project called Rustic Highlands, at Khandala.

Dada DM was short and a little rotund. His winning smile and razor-sharp mind studied a case in great depth before giving advice. His greatest talent was the art of listening which he had perfected to a fine art. With his old-world charm, he would make you sit comfortably, and then listen to every word you said. Then, in his soft voice and with a gentle smile, he would proffer advice, assuring you that he would also look at any additional documents you could provide in defence of your matter. After that, his advice was always comprehensive, taking into consideration every aspect of the case.

It was no wonder that film producers, film stars, NRIs, corporate honchos from the top echelons of business and industry – all found one address to go to for their tax matters: Dada DM's office at Marine Drive. Builders and developers still remember the days of the Voluntary Disclosure Schemes (VDS) when Dada worked tirelessly and helped so many to make declarations and resolve their tax matters.

Family and friends meant more to him than 'filthy lucre', as wealth is referred to in the Bible. A student until the last – he would sit up till late at night to make an in-depth study of a case due to come up for a hearing. And Aunty Ratni was there, supporting him at home and preparing legal briefs in the office.

I remember the days when Dada DM was representing the Scindia family of Gwalior in their Income Tax, Wealth Tax, Gold Control, FERA and other fiscal matters. He sat long hours studying every detail of the history of the Gwalior family over the last two hundred years, as the manner of succession would impact its Income Tax, Wealth Tax and Estate Duty. He then argued the matter for about five days, and succeeded. A professor of History or a research student could not have studied more!

Although he was a tax lawyer and fought many battles on behalf of his clients, he also believed in paying his taxes scrupulously. He was among the high taxpayers in the city of Bombay, and this brought him as much joy as winning the biggest cases for others.

At the age of seventy-three, Dada was advised to retire –

but instead, he did just the opposite. He worked harder than before! In addition to his professional practice, he began to write a book on Income Tax, something he had always wanted to do. This grew into an eight-volume treatise. The first volume was published on his seventy-fourth birthday and the last on his seventy-sixth. He died two months later. It was as if he had just been waiting to complete it.

Thomas Carlyle's words, "Blessed is he who has found his work," may certainly be applied to him. When I think of Dada DM, these words of Shakespeare also come to my mind:

> His life was gentle; and the elements
> So mixed in him, that Nature might stand up
> And say to all the world, This was a man!

The spirit of philanthropy which Dada DM initiated during his lifetime, by supporting innumerable students to complete their studies, has been continued by his family. The DM Harish Foundation, funded and managed by DM Harish & Co, supports various worthy causes. Dada DM always believed that moot courts were an integral part of a law student's life, and every year the Foundation arranges and sponsors the International Moot Court Competition at the Government Law College, Churchgate. Twenty to thirty teams from India and abroad participate in this annual three-day event.

Dada DM's son Anil Harish and his daughter Shobha Jagtiani are chips off the old block. Gentle in voice and courteous of manner, they too have cultivated that rare art and ability to listen patiently to every client, even when there is a long queue waiting for them. Anil was Executive Vice President of the Society of Indian Law Firms, as well as a trustee of Hyderabad Sind National Collegiate Board (HSNCB) which educates nearly 50,000 students in seventeen graduate and postgraduate colleges and eight schools, and employs around 3500 teaching and non-teaching staff. Shobha, besides her innumerable legal commitments was a member of the Legal Committee of the Indian Merchants' Chamber Ladies Wing.

Haresh Jagtiani

A lawyer and a most successful one is Haresh Jagtiani, Shobha's husband. Always in demand to teach and speak at international forums and at Law colleges in India and abroad, he was closely associated with Ram Jethmalani. Even though he found the political arena fascinating, he put aside this interest to pursue his growing legal practice and attend to his increasing line of clients.

One day in July 2020, I read a headline in *The Times of India*: Removal of Deccan Chargers: 'BCCI to pay DCHL Rs 4800 crore'.

The figure astounded me, especially since I teach in a law college. I read on. Deccan Chargers is an Indian Premier League (IPL) cricket team belonging to the Deccan Chronicle newspaper group. The Board of Control for Cricket in India (BCCI) had cancelled their contract and did not allow them to play in the IPL, and gave the right to another team.

Deccan Chronicle took the matter into arbitration. It was Haresh Jagtiani who represented *Deccan Chronicle*, and succeeded in establishing that the cancellation of their contract was mala fide and bad in law. He succeeded in getting damages of Rs4,800 crores plus interest, amounting to a total of about Rs8,000 crores, a huge victory, among the largest in India. Another Sindhi professional to be proud of, even though Haresh is not from Rohri!

The widely-read humourist, journalist and philanthropist

Will Rogers wrote:

> I don't think you can make a lawyer honest by an act of legislature. You've got to work on his conscience. And his lack of conscience is what makes him a lawyer.

While the line made me smile, I know for a fact that it is not the lack of conscience that has made the DM Harish family into successful lawyers. On the contrary it is their plenitude of conscience that has made them lawyers with a heart. That is what they are known for, and many of their clients will vouch for that. And the third generation (Dada DM's grandchildren), has already embarked on the same path.

Dr Manohar Keswani

Some years ago, a student from Iran came to me to register for his PhD degree. Since I already had my full quota of students, I suggested that he approach another recognized supervisor of the Bombay University. But he pleaded that the subject he had in mind, *Themes in the Modern Novel*, was most suited to my area of specialization. I declined and suggested the name of another professor who specialized in the same field. When he heard that this professor was affiliated to Pune university he insisted, "But, Madam, I have to stay in Bombay only, because of my treatment."

"Treatment?" I asked, suddenly concerned. He looked a fine specimen of manhood! Not wanting to sound intrusive, I asked if it was a serious problem.

He answered without hesitation: "Madam, I plan to have sex-change surgery."

Startled, I inquired in as cool a voice as I could muster: "Good idea, if you feel that way! Who is your doctor?"

"Dr MH Keswani. He has advised me psychiatric counselling for three months, and for that I have to be here in Bombay.

When I get the reports, I have to go back to Dr Keswani."

What a small world!

I had known Dr Keswani for quite some time. We worked together on a committee formed by the Association of British Council Scholars. Also, Dr Keswani is closely related by marriage to the Nain side of my family!

I knew that Dr Keswani was a highly-qualified plastic surgeon, but I did not know that this quiet, self-effacing and modest doctor performed these complicated, surgeries on the cutting edge of art, technology and social evolution! I began investigating.

Manohar Hariram Keswani was born in Sukkur in April 1931 to a wealthy and privileged family which became impoverished due to Partition. Graduating from Fergusson College in Poona in 1948, he did his professional training at The Seth Gordhandas Sunderdas Medical College and

Dr Manohar Keswani (left) greets Indian President, R Venkataraman, c1990
Image courtesy his son, Dr Sunil M Keswani

King Edward Memorial Hospital in Bombay, after which he was selected for a much-coveted post in cardio-thoracic surgery at the Christian Medical College, Vellore.

However, when he observed a Dr McPherson, who was working alone in plastic surgery at CMC, Dr Keswani's artistic impulse came to the fore and he realized that it was reconstructive surgery where his true vocation lay. It was with Dr McPherson that he learnt the basics of plastic surgery and the art of tissue handling.

Plastic surgery was new in India – glamorous and in demand. At the same time, burns was a neglected subject – most of the patients were poor and there were no established departments in the country. Dr Keswani then qualified at the best international institutes, and came back to India to set up the first paediatric burns unit in India at the Bai Jerbai Wadia Hospital for children in Bombay.

His passion for re-constructing the damage caused by burns to bodies and faces, whether they were acid burns or kitchen burns, led him to specialize in this highly innovative field – an area in which treatment was still new and uncertain. There was also an innovative side to this doctor: he boiled potato peels for making bandages which were tested and approved by research workers in Holland. And he used curds to remove damaged tissue from burn wounds.

Dr Keswani inspired Shyam Benegal and Alyque Padamsee to make films on the Prevention of Burns, films in which his message to all his patients was: "apply water to burns". Many of them had previously believed that water would make burns swell and develop blisters which would become septic.

In a fine testimonial to Dr MH Keswani, a former colleague and senior plastic surgeon Dr HS Adenwalla wrote in

Indian Journal of Plastic Surgery:

> Manohar Keswani was not a conventional plastic surgeon; neither was he a conventional man. This remarkable, self-effacing and modest individual was recognised and lauded for his work on burns. Few knew of his prowess, versatility and innovative skills in general plastic surgery. His primary and secondary cleft work, his work on hypospadias, his rhinoplasties and the fantastic results he achieved with his vaginoplasties and his pioneering sex change operation and the skill with which he could cut large skin grafts to mathematical precision will long be remembered by his close associates. I once gave him a particularly difficult secondary cleft lip correction to do. He laboured over the child for over 3 hours, undid the whole lip twice and at the end of it gave the child a lovely Cupid's bow, well-matched philtral columns, a full vermillion and a dead symmetrical nose following no set plan. At the end of it all, lost in admiration, I asked him, "How did you do it Manohar?" His answer was, "I really don't know Hirji. You saw me do it, didn't you?" He was improvising all the time, and drawing heavily, I think, on past experience.
>
> It is little known that he had published several slim volumes of poetry. A connoisseur of art, he had both the hand and the heart of an artist. Above all, I shall remember him as a gentleman par excellence, patient, caring, kind and ethical to the core.

In 2002, Dr Keswani ventured on a gigantic project, against the advice of his friends and well-wishers who believed it was impossible for one man to complete what he had in mind. With tremendous perseverance and courage, and sinking his own meagre resources in it, he founded the National Burns Centre at Airoli in New Bombay. It was

2007 when he died.

Today, the National Burns Centre is the largest specialized burns hospital in India, and a lasting legacy of this exceptional doctor. As for me – if I ever accidentally scald my hand while cooking, I immediately hold the affected part under a tap of running water. Or if that is not possible, I dab the seared portion with a handkerchief dipped in water. And in just a few minutes there is no trace of injury. Thank you, Dr Manohar Keswani of Rohri-Sukkur!

8. Shikarpur: sometimes a hundi is more useful than a cookpot

It is a fact of life that you need money to start a business. And when you have no money but have to start a business – you can only do it by borrowing. For our mercantile community, the complex and reliable system that the Shikarpuri hundis provided, were to the businessman like water to a fish.

When I first heard the word 'hundi', I thought it was the kitchen utensil being referred to! Then, going back in time, I remembered an occasion when a friend of my father's, who was about to start a business, was sorely in need of a small loan. He looked dejected for days when friends and family informed him that he couldn't possibly be a suitable candidate for a bank loan as the paperwork was intimidating and it also required him to furnish a guarantor and provide collateral, neither of which he could. Then my father introduced him to his Shikarpuri friend – after which everything worked out smoothly.

Being a professor of English, the system of the hundi and how it operated was not very clear to me. I was more familiar with Shakespeare's lines

> Neither a borrower nor a lender be
> For loan oft loses both itself and he

which the Shikarpuris would hotly contest – for the Bard's perceptive observation would be a severe blow to the source of their business and livelihood! They would surely turn around with a rebuttal in the poet's own words,

There are more things in heaven and earth,
Horatio, than are dreamt of in your philosophy!

When I had the opportunity to observe another hundi transaction take place, it seemed to me like a miracle. IRB's Gujarati friend had a problem: he wished to purchase an apartment but did not have the funds to make the down payment, for which a date had been set. He confided to IRB that there was another contender waiting with ready means to purchase the much-coveted apartment. IRB in his usual confident manner told him to relax. With one phone call the work was done, and the Gujarati friend was able to put the money on the table that same evening.

No documents, no collateral!

I thought the 'hundi' must be some wonder drug when I saw the Gujarati friend flushed with happiness that evening.

In time, I learnt that the system worked not only in Bombay but across the world. And that it was the Sindhi Shikarpuris who were masters of this 'hundi' phenomenon.

Colloquially defined, the hundi is a bill of exchange, a sound and reliable method of remittance used to settle debts and transfer funds. The credit-worthiness of the borrower is known to the lender through his vast but tightly-networked business circle, and the transaction is conducted quickly. The borrowing is at a higher rate of interest, but far less laborious than the time and money spent in providing documents and guarantors as required for loans from traditional banks. During the colonial period too, the British Government was reluctant to interfere with this system as they considered it an essential cog of the Indian economy.

When I read Alexander Burnes's book *Travels into Bukhara* (1834), I saw how convenient the system had proved for him. Travelling from Karachi to Kabul, the hundis easily extended by Shikarpuri bankers made it possible for him to collect cash at Bukhara, Astrakhan and other places where he needed it, without the risk of carrying large sums on the route which proliferated with bandits. All he had to do was show a note, and currency was advanced to him.

Robert Burton too wrote about Shikarpur as "a place of almost Asiatic fame, on account of the mercantile speculations and extensive banking influence of its adventurous natives" (1844). Thomas Postans refers to Shikarpur as "the great mart of Sindh" (1843). And Claude Markovits wrote, "Shikarpur in the second half of the eighteenth century appears to have been a kind of bania 'melting pot', where merchants of different origins established a residence" (2001).

An advanced city

Shikarpur's history dates back to the early seventeenth century when it became a hub of trade because of its strategic position on an arterial trade route. This was when financially sharp and innovative migrants from surrounding provinces settled there and formed the basis of our Shikarpuri community. Their trade network spread between Iran, Iraq, Samarkand, Burma, Sumatra, Japan, and other places. Through this, the Shikarpuri bankers brought considerable wealth back and contributed generously towards the development of their city.

One of the significant initiatives was made in 1927 by Chelasingh Satramdas and Sitaldas Tirathdas Punjabi, who registered the Upper Sindh College Association. Some of their associates are named by the present administrators of the college as "Thakur Das, Narain Das, Professor Shewaram Pherwani, Seth Dolat Ram, Seth Shol Das, Dr Bhagwan Das, Dr Kishanchand, Deewan Wadhomal,

Verho Mal Gokilani, and Phago Mal"[1]. The college was inaugurated by HT Sorley, Collector of Sukkur, in June 1933. In 1937, it was moved to a newly constructed building which had been planned and constructed by Chelasingh and Sitaldas. They contributed funds and also collected donations from other philanthropists of Shikarpur, Sultankot, Sukkur, Rohiri, Larkana, Dadu, Jacobabad and Quetta. The college was a boon for the development of Shikarpur as it offered higher education to students who, until then, would have had to go to Karachi or further off, to Bombay, to study after their schooling.

Another Hindu trader and philanthropist, devastated when his mother fell ill and could not be saved, contributed Rs100,000 to build a modern hospital with good doctors that provided free service, food and medicines. It was named after him: the Udhavdas Tarachand Hospital.

Yet another Shikarpuri businessman set up a private power plant which gave the city uninterrupted electricity. An underground drainage system kept the city clean. There are still many elderly Shikarpuris in India today who remember their city's Dhak Bazaar, a long, covered bazaar shaded by a roof made of fine teak wood. This kept the bazaar cool even in summer.

Well-known artists, singers and litterateurs naturally loved to visit a place like this, and the Shikarpuris, a cultured, affluent and generous social group made excellent patrons.

When Pakistan was formed, the Chelasingh Sitaldas College was renamed CNS Government College. In 1948-49, there were just forty-eight students, as most of the students had been Hindus and they had fled with their families across the new border.

---

1 https://www.shikarpurparisofsindh.com/2020/04/c-government-degree-college-shikarpur.html

Udhavdas Tarachand hospital, Shikarpur c1940, with the statue of Rai Bahadur Udhavdas Tarachand in front of it
Image courtesy Seth Udhavdas Tarachand's great-grandson, Nandu Asrani

Udhavdas Tarachand hospital still stands in Shikarpur today, but the statue of Seth Udhavdas Tarachand was removed to protect it from rioters, and kept safely in Jamshoro University, Hyderbad, where it remains.

When the Hindus left Shikarpur, the building and city infrastructure decayed. Grand old homes were occupied by poor migrants and became overcrowded and were not maintained. The expensive fittings of carpentry, metal and glass were stripped and can be found in large furniture bazaars around Pakistan or under the hammer at art auctions, even today. Some are reported to have been fitted into the fancy restaurants of the city.

Unfaithful spouses

Writers and critics on Shikarpur have emphasized the unfaithfulness of Shikarpuri wives who were left behind for long periods of time while the husbands were away on trade and business. According to Richard Burton, whose provocative comments are sometimes to be taken with a pinch of salt, they were ready and willing to have a man come and warm their beds. On the husband's return, he would see his repentant wife surrounded by a bevy of little ones who could not have been his. After some obligatory reprimanding, the husband accepted his attractive and sweet-tongued wife – and her offspring too!

Markovits writes of the second establishments set up by the Shikarpuri seths themselves in the places they lived for years at a time. Back at home, too, they were known to set up separate establishments for their mistresses. While these are commonplace acts of wealthy men of every community around the world, Burton's description of the women and children shows an enviable modernity among the families of Shikarpur more than a hundred years ago!

Entrance to the Bolan Pass from Dadur

Plate 5 from *Sketches in Afghaunistan* by James Atkinson, Superintending Surgeon of the Army of the Indus, that marched on Kabul in 1839.

My family's Shikarpuri connection

It was Langley's description of Shikarpur that brought memories rolling at full speed into my mind. Langley wrote:

> Shikarpoor is situated on the high road to Candahar by the Bolan Pass, and this must always give it an important influence on the trade of the Indus and the countries beyond.

The words 'Bolan Pass' and 'Kandahar' struck bells in my mind.

My father travelled often from Quetta through the Bolan Pass to the countries beyond. With his cargo of tea chests, supplied to him by Parmanand Deepchand Hinduja from east India, and dry fruits and other sundry articles, he proceeded to Isfahan, Tehran, Kabul, Kazi Dera Khan, the Khyber Pass, and other places. A young and enterprising trader, he made good profits, and it was on these trading trips that he became fluent in Pashto, Persian and Urdu.

In the past, people travelled on horseback, camelback or in caravans through the Bolan Pass which had been cut through the mountain ranges to provide a shortcut to the North West Frontier. Plans for a railway line had been drawn up by the British authorities as early as 1876 but the mountainous territory and harsh weather conditions caused work to proceed slowly and it was only in 1886 that a steam engine moved through the Bolan Pass into Quetta from Afghanistan. My father travelled through the Pass to Afghanistan sometimes by road and sometimes by rail.

Present-day royalty

When Partition took place in 1947, my family left by sea from Karachi and arrived at Jam Khambalia. My uncle Justice JL Nain, who had joined the British Navy as a short-term officer, arranged for us to travel by steamer from Karachi to Gujarat. This had been difficult, as there were multitudes anxiously waiting to escape the newly-formed Pakistan and enter the safety of India, but he had managed. Then, a few days after our arrival at Jam Khambalia, my father made a spontaneous decision. Most members of our extended

Parmanand Deepchand Hinduja (1901-1971) and
Mrs Jamuna Parmanand Hinduja (1904-1973)

family were heading to Bombay. But my father decided to travel with us to Calcutta. Calcutta was the centre of the Indian tea industry, and he knew he would be able to continue his business from there.

Mr Parmanand had two flats in a building in No 1, Moti Sil Street in central Calcutta, and a *pedhi* or office in the same building. He generously invited us to come and stay in his vacant flat until we could figure out our next step. He also permitted my father to use his postal address to start his business. For my father, with a young family to take care of, this was indeed a blessing.

Fortunately, we soon found an apartment in a building across the road at No 46, Moti Sil Street, and moved there. He continued his tea business with Mr Parmanand, who travelled quite often to Iran for his own investments. I remember Mr Jhangaldas, also a Shikarpuri, who looked after Mr Parmanand's *pedhi* in his absence. His family stayed in the same building, and they too were very supportive and ever ready to help my young mother with her four small kids.

It was later that I heard from my family that Mr Parmanand's business extended across several cities and his family had close ties with the Shah of Iran. He even exported Raj Kapoor films to Iran, perhaps creating the craze for Raj Kapoor in Iran and other countries.

Tea at Hinduja House

For old time's sake, I met Mr Ashok Hinduja over a cup of coffee at Hinduja House in Bombay recently, a beautiful glass-fronted building which overlooks the sea and the Haji Ali Dargah. We spoke nostalgically about our old memories of Calcutta and the close family ties. My father had been in touch with Mr Parmanand, the family patriarch, until he passed away in 1971, at the age of seventy. It was obvious that Mr Ashok Hinduja cherished his father's old friendships. As we chatted, we discovered other common friends too. Time flew until I realized I had already spent over an hour in his office and it was time for me to leave.

Of Mr Parmanand's four sons, Ashok is the youngest. He spends time in Bombay, overseeing the family's Indian interests. Srichand and Gopichand live in London, while Prakash resides in Switzerland.

The Hinduja home in London is Carlton House Terrace, near Buckingham Palace, overlooking St James's Park. Once the boyhood home of King George IV, it was the Hindujas who purchased it once it went under the hammer, beating bids from Russian and Middle Eastern – and Indian – billionaires. This mansion has four six-storey Georgian houses, all inter-connected for this traditional Shikarpuri joint family of four brothers and their families. At the entranceway stands an imposing statue of Queen Victoria. Is she looking daggers at these Sindhis from her former colonies?

Across the road, they own another four-floor 25,000 square-foot flat. And not too far away, close to No 10, Downing Street and Westminster Abbey, is the building occupied by Winston Churchill as a War Office during the World War, and now in the process of being converted by the Hinduja brothers into London's finest luxury destination in partnership with Raffles Hotels and Resorts of Singapore. So the acquisition of the Buckingham Palace, the official residence of the Queen of England, may not be far off!

Today, the Hinduja Group has become one of the largest diversified groups in the world spanning every continent. The Group employs over 150,000+ people. Their flagship company Ashok Leyland is the second-largest manufacturer of commercial vehicles in India, the fourth largest manufacturer of buses in the world, and the tenth largest manufacturer of trucks globally. The company has offices in fifty countries, and its headquarters are in Chennai. It has nine manufacturing plants around the world, with seven manufacturing plants in India and one each in UAE and Leeds, England.

One of the best-known initiatives of the Hinduja Group are the Hinduja hospitals in Bombay, known for their advanced medical facilities and highly qualified staff. The Group also runs the P D Hinduja College of Nursing, which was entrusted to the care of Mrs Lalita Girdhar Hinduja when she was widowed at a young age. Parmanand Deepchand encouraged her to move on with her life rather than just follow the regressive tradition of mourning and isolation. She took up the responsibility, and turned his vision for an independent nursing and education centre into a reality. The NAAC-accredited 'A' Grade P D Hinduja College of Nursing is the institution she nurtured, fulfilling her father-in-law's dream.

Onions and potatoes

After the patriarch passed away, my father lost touch with the family. However, his memories remained. One of the stories my father loved to tell us was about how, in the early 1970s, the Hindujas rushed to the help of the Shah of Iran with huge supplies of potatoes and onions.

Why? The booming Iranian economy with rising global oil prices and overcrowded ports had brought a lot of money but at the same time, a severe food crisis. So the Shah immediately contacted the Hinduja brothers, his aggressive and spirited friends, knowing that they would help him to find a solution. And they did – by filling each and every town and city of Iran with potatoes and onions, which satisfied the demand and brought prices down to affordable levels. The onions and potatoes were sourced from Amritsar and Jalandhar, where it seems there had been a bumper crop. All the Hindujas had to do was to buy the surplus in the Indian Punjab, transport it through Pakistan to Zahedan, and then over the border into Iranian Balochistan. From there, local distribution networks would quickly glut the local markets, causing prices to drop.

There was just one hitch to this neat plan. No Indian trucks had been allowed on Pakistan's roads since the country

The Hinduja brothers, Prakash, Srichand, Gopichand, and Ashok, at their office in Bombay
Image courtesy Ashish Ahuja

was created in 1947 by partitioning India.

The Hindujas discussed the matter with the Pakistani premier at the time, Zulfikar Ali Bhutto. Perhaps they discussed the matter with him in Sindhi, since that was his native tongue as much as theirs! He gave his permission. However, Indian truck drivers would not be given Pakistan visas. So the Hindujas had a new project: they had to get approximately 1400 non-Indian truck drivers capable of driving loaded trucks through the challenging route their convoy needed to take. They contacted international agencies, who flew in reliable drivers, and in just three weeks, the exercise of moving potatoes and onions by road was successfully completed and the food crisis abated.

Quick-thinking is doubtless one of the attributes that helped the Hindujas to become one of the richest families in the world. I sometimes wonder whether their vegetarianism is another! After all, two of the other wealthiest Indian families, the Ambanis and the Mittals, are also strict vegetarians. Perhaps this will be my next research project, to see if there is indeed some relevance to the proposition!

The Hindujas are a particularly devout family. Prayer is an important part of each one's daily routine. They also support religious institutions such as the Khatwari Darbar in Khar, a centre for community worship and also a place that made valiant attempts, until recently, to teach Sindhi to children. 'Khatta' means cot in Sindhi and the Khatwari Darbar of Shikarpur was so named because in Shikarpur it had a cot made of gold. Rich offerings were made by the devout and it gained in importance because supposedly its originator Baba Gurdas, was said to have the miraculous power of turning sand into sugar.

Besides community support, the Hinduja brothers have

long striven to assist the needy as their father did during the Partition period. My family and other relatives still remember the care and hospitality they received during those difficult days.

Yes, Sindhis have been adept at 'making money' and this brings to my mind Somerset Maugham's comment – refreshingly contrary to the derogatory comments generally more prevalent – that unless one has the sixth sense to make money, one cannot make good use of the other five senses.

The Hindujas clearly do have this sixth sense! And the money made is often used for philanthropy, and a legacy of trusts for education and healthcare for the underprivileged.

9. A MOST IMPORTANT SEARCH

I had just turned twenty-two, and was about to appear for my final MA exams in a week's time. I had noticed that both my mother and father had been looking tense. I put it down to my erratic behaviour: I would get up at 4am and study all morning. In the afternoon, I would announce I wasn't going to appear for the exam. These theatrics took place during the peak of Calcutta's historical 'load-shedding' era. When I wanted to study there was no electricity and it was the month of May, and 42°C in the shade! All this added to my woes, and my parents' tolerance levels were also showing cracks.

On one of my worst days, I had finally dozed off. My sister Mira, a medical student, would not be returning home that evening (with her usual baggage of dissected toads and cockroaches and other such creepy-crawly creatures) because some well-known medical personage was conducting a high-level demonstration in her college lab and attendance was compulsory. She had phoned – not an easy act in those days when she would have had to stand in line at the college office, perhaps also having got permission in writing to use its hallowed phone – to warn me that I must under NO condition touch the thirty-three bones of the vertebral column she had painstakingly assembled on the dining table.

She had been suspecting that, over the last two months, I had been venting my frustration with the long-winded narration of the battles of Beowulf and the countless sexual exploits of Chaucer's *Wife of Bath* on the innumerable bones of the human skeleton which lay strewn around the house. She had even discovered a hair-line fracture on the clavicle, which I had been using as a paper weight. Mine was an era when Old English and Middle English were still considered mandatory, having been prescribed by the Bengali Brown Sahibs of Calcutta University, who considered the word of the old British academics to be the word of God!

So Mira would be spending the night in her college hostel, having dined on half-cooked food from the Calcutta Medical College canteen. And my parents assumed I was fast asleep. And then I heard an interesting conversation.

"Now we must speed up the search," mother was saying.

"Yes of course. You think I'm not searching. I'm looking around and searching everywhere all the time"

"I don't see you searching. You are always so busy with your tea samples and your tea garden affairs." A complaining tone had crept into my mother's reply.

"I'm surprised that you still haven't realized after all these years what a thoroughly well-organized man I am! But I do have to concentrate on the business as well!" responded father, provoked to border-line belligerence.

"I know, I know," said mother soothing him, "I know how hard you worked when we arrived in Calcutta after Partition. You had already started making notes in your diary. And you had already started looking for the best schools, even though the children were still so small. Baby Mira was just one! As soon as you could spare some time and money, you went all the way to Shantiniketan to see the school set up by Tagore and decide whether we should send the girls there. You wanted the best for them, and you always planned everything meticulously."

"We had to. We came as refugees. You know each day was a day of struggle: looking for a roof over our heads, getting a foot-hold in the tea market, attending to the children and arranging for their school admissions," said father, his voice softening, "But God has helped us, Parvati."

I wondered whether I should get up and tell them I was awake and could help them with the 'search', even though I wasn't clear about what they were searching for.

I had often heard Father narrate the story of how he had wound a belt around his waist – a belt ingeniously stuffed with gold guineas and cash – before we fled Pakistan after Partition. He had managed to sell his tea warehouse and a few other assets, with the help of an old English friend, when the political turmoil in Quetta became violent.

After wrapping the belt around his waist, he had put on his underwear and then his trousers. His outer garment was a loose bush shirt which he could only hope was concealing everything. People fleeing from the chaos that ensued after Partition was declared, and which worsened after Pakistan was created, were being threatened and robbed and killed for their valuables.

We were so fortunate to have escaped safely, travelling from Quetta to Karachi and embarking on the steamship Sonavati to Jam Khambalia. Here we stayed in a home close to the railway station. The new Government of India had made some provision here to accommodate and feed the hordes of incoming refugees arriving by sea from Karachi in army camps and other government buildings. Fortunately, my father had worked with Kajaria Marbles in Quetta, and they provided us with a roof over our heads until we could make further plans.

The secret pocket

In Calcutta too, where we settled after Partition, Father designed a secret pocket stitched to his underwear. Whenever he had to carry money and valuables, or when he was travelling, he would put his precious stuff into the concealed pocket. With instructions from my father, my mother also stitched secret pockets in the clothes we children wore for our out-of-town school trips. Even if we lost our luggage, they reckoned, we would always have our cash intact.

To this day I feel positively uncomfortable and uneasy if I don't have my secret pocket when I am travelling. I wear undergarments which have pockets. Recently during a college trip with students to Rashtrapati Bhavan in Delhi, my students and I had to go through a security check at the entry point, the kind of thorough check I have never experienced before. The lady security officer immediately felt the bulge in my saree petticoat and questioned me.

"Madam, what are you carrying?" she asked suspiciously, "You know nothing is permitted to be taken into Rashtrapati Bhavan." She probably suspected a gun or a bomb!

"I am carrying 30,000 rupees in the secret pocket of my saree petticoat. If there is an emergency, I am responsible for the well-being of my students."

Perhaps I have an honest face, because she did not make me undress and show her the money, but let me pass through!

The secret pocket must have been a device that made us refugees feel secure in times of distress. The anxiety of dislocation which we faced, I think, brought about some change in our genetic structure. And this trait has passed on to the next generation as well. For I have noticed, my daughter Vandana always manages to contrive a secret compartment in the base of her handbag, where she stows away some cash for use in an emergency.

Father's diary

I was half-dozing when I heard my father's voice again. Then I saw him pick up his bedside diary and say: "I have already done some searching."

"Tell me quickly. *Der ahey andher na ahey,*" said mother happily. When my parents were agitated or excited or happy, they always expressed themselves in old-fashioned Sindhi *pahakas*. They had one for almost every occasion, and what my mother now said used darkness as a metaphor implying that there had been a delay, but not despair. In later years, I found that IRB too would also revert to *pahakas* when he wanted to explain his point lucidly. The two he used most often were:

Ba ta barah: when there are two people together to face a difficult situation, they are as strong and capable as a dozen.

Païse palo mahango, rüpaye sasto: an expensive item seems less expensive when you have plenty of money.

And now my mother came up with another.

"*Jao ta ahey*: He has already been born … he exists!"

And this was when I realized what it was they were searching for. A groom for me!

Choosing the right one

"You know Gobind, of course," said my father, "He is a part of my morning walkers' group. He was recently in Bombay to visit his sisters. They told him there is a most eligible boy. He resides in Bombay, that is where most of the affluent Sindhis live. He is Shikarpuri, and he has …"

Mother waved her hands in dismissal.

"Please," she said, "you know we Sahiti people don't give our girls to Shikarpuris, affluent or not. Shikarpuris are all money-lenders and their main business is hundis. Neither

A traditionally-dressed Shikarpuri family, painted from memory of his parents and himself as a child in Shikarpur, by Menghraj Talreja.

Collection of Saaz Aggarwal

the parents nor their children are educated. Rule him out."

"Why don't you listen, Parvati! This boy is educated. Don't you know that the younger generation of Sindhis has been getting educated?"

"No, no! Their manners and customs are different. Even their language sounds different. And their *saee bhajī* is different from ours. And they only talk about money. And some of them still wear dhotis and topis and sit in their *pedhīs*. They haven't advanced. Imagine the father-in-law at the wedding, sitting next to you in a dhoti!" said my mother coldly.

"Ok, ok," said father, "but I don't know why you are so averse to our traditional Indian dress."

"Well your elder brother Dada, who happens to be my *bhen-e-vīyo* and *daera*, my older sister's husband and your brother as well – is a High Court Judge. He is going to be suited and booted and will definitely not like this Shikarpuri sitting near him in the same photo wearing a dhoti!"

"Well, we can tell the father-in-law to put on a suit," said father helpfully.

"Really! You don't know anything about customs. We will be the girl's side. You can't dictate terms to the boy's side and tell the father-in-law what to do and what not to do. In all probability you will have to wear a dhoti or *sūthan* and *jhabba* like men used to wear in Sindh! Then!"

"Then what!" said my father, laughing.

"I told you – just leave the Shikarpuri out," said my mother firmly.

"Well then let me look at my diary. I'll tell you about the boy Dada recommended in his last letter. The boy is from a good Amil family and has a job in a bank. He is educated and his father was an engineer in Hyderabad."

"These Amils think themselves to be God's gift to humanity because they were munshis and clerks to the Muslims and to the British. They knew English and Persian. But now they

Lokumal (1914–1999) and Parvati Nain (1924–1983), the author's parents, soon after their marriage in 1940

are mostly in service and their main business is reminding everyone of how superior they are! And they will make our daughter miserable. No, no Amils if we can help it."

"My dear Parvati, at this rate we will never get our daughter married! She will finish her MA in another month and then …"

"Then what! Amils are tight-fisted. These bureaucrats all share that common habit. They will eat a meal at a restaurant together, and then wait for others to pay. Forget Amils. I'll prefer even a wine-selling Baluchi Bhagnari to an Amil."

"You really mean you don't mind Bhagnaris?" my father asked in astonishment.

"I'm just using a comparison," she replied quickly. "I'm not approving or disapproving of Bhagnaris and their business. I love their khatti dal and their dishes spiced with dry fruits. Their Saraiki language is of course a little different from the way we speak Sindhi."

"Well, then, there is this Sindhworki boy …" said father looking into his diary again.

"My God, are you really thinking of a Sindhworki for our daughter?" she asked in horror. "You know they go away for three to four years on *musafri* and God knows how many mistresses and illegitimate children they have. It's so difficult to find out who they have been living with. You can't expect a virile young man to remain celibate when he is alone and far away on a three-year *musafri*. He must be having a mistress in Hong Kong or Singapore or wherever he is posted. How will we be able to find out?"

"All that is changing now, my dear. Some of them are in better positions nowadays, and the managers are allowed to take their wives with them. Also you know our Sindhi boys are very enterprising. After three or four years they manage to start a business or a shop of their own."

"No, no, my gut tells me not to give my daughter to a Sindhworki! They are always flaunting their gold and their diamonds and bragging about their Black Label Whisky."

"This Sindhworki boy is an educated MBA," said my father confidently.

"Must be an MBA from some 'faltoo' (second rate) university. What do Sindhworkis know about education!"

"Parvati, you are of the opinion that only Sahiti people are the best! The Bhagnaris all deal in liquor, the Brahmans are backward, the Shikarpuris only think of money, the Amils suffer from a superiority complex, the Bhaibands ..."

"Yes, why don't you look for Bhaibands, Thattaees and people from Rohri? And not the Sindhworki Bhaibands, please. Let us find a boy from a family of Bhaiband Seths of Karachi."

"Where do I look for the famous Bhaiband Seths of Karachi?"

"My friend knows the family. I'll find out. We have two beautiful daughters. One is a topper at every university exam and the other is going to be a brilliant doctor! They are both fair and beautiful – as you say due to our Greek blood which we inherited when Alexander's soldiers settled down in Sindh on the banks of the Indus ..."

"Yes Parvati, you are right, as usual. But it will be like looking for a needle in a haystack."

"I know who to talk to," said my mother confidently.

At this point, though my fate was being decided and sealed, I must have dozed off, for I didn't hear the rest of the conversation. (As you may have guessed, this was the lead that brought IRB into my family: Indru R Bharvani, my husband!)

10. None of us

are children of a lesser god

The most wonderful thing about us Sindhis is that we are not oppressed by the caste system that plagues Hindus across India. All human beings are treated as equals. Women are treated with respect. No one is looked upon as the child of a lesser God. When I think of my advanced and liberated community, Gandhi's words come to my mind: "The purification required is not of untouchables, but of the so-called superior castes."

The general term used by the British to encompass Hindu society in Sindh was 'Lohana'. Lohana is sometimes taken to mean 'Descendants of Luv', Luv being the son of the Hindu god, Ram. He was portrayed as a warrior, a master of swords. Another version ascribes their origins to the community of Rathor Rajputs. When Raja Jaichand of Kanauj declared war against them, they prayed to Lord Varuna, who secured them in a spiritual fort, from which they were able to battle to victory. They built a real fort of iron, Lohghar, at the site and consequently came to be known as Lohanas. The only non-Lohana Hindus were the Brahmans and the tribals of the Tharparkar districts.

Though there is no caste system among us Sindhis, we have distinct communities with different cultural and professional or regional characteristics. People of lower Sindh, under the urban influence of Hyderabad and Karachi and with a larger number of schools and colleges, considered themselves more sophisticated. In upper

Sindh, around Sehwan, Sukkur, Larkana and Shikarpur, the dialect differed.

The Sindhi communities tend to be free-flowing and open, and people could pass from one to another by changing their place or profession, and adapting. Roughly, they were:

Amils: The word comes from 'amal', which means 'to administer'. Amils were proficient in Persian, and worked in the administration of the Moghul rulers and the Mirs. When the British conquered Sindh, they took to the education introduced by the new rulers, were quick to learn the English language, and were soon appointed as bureaucrats in the British government. Working in positions of importance, they gave themselves airs and announced that they were the superior class.

Bhaibands: This was the business class engaged in trading and business activities. But there was no hard and fast division. Sometimes one member of a family may have been a trader while another may have been in service.

Sahiti-ja: Originating in the region called Sahiti, they too considered education of utmost importance, and had teachers, doctors, and engineers in their families.

Sindhworkis: Those Bhaibands who travelled out of Sindh to trade and sell articles made in Sindh were called Sindhworkis. The earliest products they traded were of 'Sindhwork' – handicrafts of Sindh including muslins, fine materials, embroidered goods, hand-crafted wooden articles and other things which were popular in areas outside Sindh. In 1869, when the Suez Canal opened, travel became easier and the Sindhworkis flourished.

Chhaprus: The word Chhappar means 'mountain'. This community stayed in the mountainous regions of Sindh and later many came to settle in Karachi.

Bhatias were worshippers of Lord Krishna. They are one of the oldest business communities of Sindh, trading between Thatta and the Gulf.

Thakurs were the official Brahmans of the Sindhi community.

Bhagnaris came from two small villages in Sindh: Bhag and Nari. Hence called themselves 'Bhagnaris'.

Masands followed Sikhism and spread the word of the fourth Guru, Guru Ramdas.

Brahmans were not considered high caste but merely as performing a service and they were few in number. The lack of Brahman domination in Sindh is sometimes explained by the theory that when Alexander the Great came to Sindh, the Brahmans advised the rulers not to greet the Greek invaders. As a punishment the Greeks massacred the Brahmans. Another story says that in the twelfth century, Muhammad bin Qasim defeated Hindu King Dahir with the aid of disloyal Brahmans. When Muhammad bin Qasim came to power, he executed the Brahmans whom he had experienced as disloyal people.

Marriages between these different communities were not uncommon. Of course the first preference was always to marry from the same 'jaati'. Amils did not mind giving their daughters in marriage to a boy from a Bhaiband family as the Bhaiband families were generally prosperous. But Bhaiband girls normally did not choose to marry Amil boys with limited service incomes. Besides, Bhaiband mothers-in-law were wary of having an educated daughter-in-law with an independent streak! Today, however, most of our children do not know which Sindhi sub-community they belong to – and they usually don't care, either!

11. Nani, the Beautiful Begum

Soon after our marriage my mother-in-law (IRB's mother) told us to visit her mother (IRB's nani) who stayed quite close by in a large sea-facing flat at Nanik Niwas on Warden Road, with her two sons, two daughters-in-law and several little grandkids.

A small diversion here will not be out of place.

After Partition, enterprising Sindhis aware of the pressing need of the community for housing, went into the business of constructing cooperative housing societies, primarily for their own displaced brethren. By the time the needs of the community had been satisfied, they had realized that it had the potential for an extremely lucrative business, and many Sindhis took the opportunity. In most parts of Bombay – from Chembur to Colaba – there are cooperative housing societies set up by Sindhis. Close to nani's Nanik Niwas are Shyam Niwas and Sukhmani, both large housing complexes where the original residents were mostly Sindhis. These societies were designed to have space for a Gurmandar, as we Nanakpanthi Sindhis call our temples. The Gurmandar was used not only for traditional rituals during festivals, but also for family events such

Our Nani, the beautiful begum
Image courtesy Bina Hemrajani

as marriages, **mŭndan** and thread ceremonies, and prayers for the departed. Even today, many families who will host a celebratory get-together at a five-star hotel or fashionable resort, will do so only after a prayer service in the Gurmandar.

Nani, now seventy-five, was lying comfortably on her bed. She looked beautifully gracious in her glistening white saree, hennaed hair and with **sŭrma** lining her eyes. Reclining like one of those classic aristocratic begums adorned in fine muslin, she was the perfect picture of a live model for a miniature Moghul painting.

I had once asked Nani if it was not troublesome to apply **mendī** on her hair regularly and she had explained, "I always applied it in Karachi, just like my Muslim friends did. Now it is a habit. And so is the **sŭrma**. My Muslim friends used to pound the **sŭrma** in a silver pestle on a moonlit night. We believed that the moon's rays are good for eyesight. See – I am still able to read my *Hindvasi* Sindhi newspaper every day!"

The Dive

I touched Nani's feet to seek her blessings as also did IRB. With his old-fashioned charm, IRB always said "Jai Maharaj" while diving down. Nani smiled graciously and said "**chhŭt**" (bless you) as is customary among Bhaibands.

Before my marriage, I had been instructed by my Sahiti family that I must bow down to mother-in-law and father-in-law every morning and night. Mother-in-law enjoyed this custom and I could see the smug look of glee on her face as she said "**chhŭt**". But father-in-law, educated and liberal in his views, told me softly with his gentle smile on the first day, "You may follow this custom with your mother-in-law. Leave me out."

There was a standing joke between IRB and me in the early days of our marriage. When I lay down beside him at night he would laugh and ask, "Have you performed for your mother-in-law? Get that out of the way first! Otherwise you are going to remember suddenly and jump up and run to her and I wouldn't be able to bear that!"

Nani was now seventy-five, but age had not withered her; neither had custom staled her infinite variety! She had given birth to my mother-in-law in the first flush of her marriage. Then there was a long break. Very long. Years later, after her daughter (my mother-in-law) got married and begot a son, my IRB, Nani – or was it Nana – got the mechanics going and Nani delivered four sons in quick succession. And bottom line: IRB had four mamas close to him in age.

With the generations all mixed up as happens in such cases, IRB was often nursed by Nani, and she was as fond of him as any mother would be of her own son.

We sat down, and Nani called out to her maid, Shantibai, to push our chairs closer to her bed so that she would have no difficulty in hearing us. As soon as we sat down, she drew IRB close to her and planted a kiss on his forehead, laughed, and asked in a loud stage whisper:

"**Pŭtt-a**, you like her, don't you?"

IRB smiled and coyly nodded his head. Then she said loudly,

"You boys are all the same. First you say 'No, no, no, no,' to marriage. And then after marriage, you cannot bear to leave your wives even for a single night."

Then glancing at me coquettishly, she asked, "**Kŭaar**, I am right, aren't I?"

I looked embarrassed. She gave IRB another bear hug, chiding him gently, "I'm so glad you agreed to get married. Your mother tells me you don't give her permission to go and spend even one night with her aunt who stays nearby."

IRB laughed and replied, "No Nani, that is not true! I gave her permission to go! But she didn't want to go. What could I do?"

We all laughed and Nani said happily, "Khush raho, khush raho!" Then she called out to her maid:

"Where are you, you mūee?" You become invisible when I need you. Mūee, come soon and bring some snacks!"

"Nani don't ask her to get anything. We are on our way to visit a friend and are going out for dinner after that. But you go ahead and have something. It is your tea time, Nani."

"Pūtt-a, I hardly eat anything nowadays. Jee khūsh ta jahan khūsh. I have sehko all the time."

"Why Nani? asked IRB, "What do you eat in the mornings?"

"Nothing! Absolutely nothing! I have my bath. I sit on the chair and that muee Shanti, who has no Shanti, babbles all the time instead of helping me with my towel and my clothes. Such a kaamchor – lazy lout – she is! Then I do my shewa, keep flowers and agarbati in my puja room and ..."

"Nani, I remember you always used to read Guru Granth Sahib after your bath. Don't you read it now?

"Of course, pūtt-a, if I don't read my two pages of the Granth Sahib in the morning, then for the whole day I feel miserable. I thank Guru Baba that I have good eyesight because of my sūrm-a and I can still read my Gurmukhi."

"Yes, I remember Nani, you used to try to teach it to me too until I went away to my boarding school in Panchgani!"

"Yes, you children never learnt Gurmukhi and you never

learnt Sindhi! Times changed. You were all sent to English schools! My cousin Gurbi – she is nearly eighty-five and also ailing – has told me that if she passes away, I must not throw away her Granth Sahib. None of her children read Gurmukhi. She says I must get it bound properly, wrap it in a silk cloth and give it as an offering to the Gurdwara. I have promised to do that for her if I am still alive. Otherwise **pŭtt-a**, you will have to do that, with both the Granths, hers and mine! **Kŭaar**, you must remind him."

I nodded my head.

Nani changed her position on the bed, exclaiming, "What to do? I also have **moonjh** and **sehko** all the time."

"What do you eat in the mornings, Nani?" repeated IRB.

"**Pŭtt-a**, after reading my Granth Sahib, I only have my prasad. Nothing else. I have taught that **mŭee** Shanti to make prasad – one katori of dry fruits, one katori of sooji ka seera and only one glass of milk Sometimes I have a papad and ..."

"Nani," said IRB, "Your breakfast is too heavy. That is why you experience **moonjh** and **sehko**."

"But **pŭtt-a**, it is prasad only. That is something I always used to have in Karachi. There we had our own cows and milk, and such good homemade ghee. But now I have to manage with whatever is there."

"Nani, you were young then and you could digest all that ghee. Not now!" advised IRB.

"But I have so much **godan jo soor** – knee pain all the time. My body needs this oil. Otherwise how will I move about? My bones are all drying up, and ..."

"Nani you must walk and do some exercise. I will ask my friend at Bhatia Hospital to send you a physiotherapist to make you do some easy exercises for **godan jo soor**.

Then you will also be able to lose some weight and there will be less pressure on your knees."

"No, no exercise please, pŭtt-a. Don't even talk about it, " said Nani firmly, "at my age if I have to jump around and dance like you, I will die!" Then touching her knees, "Aaee Allah! I have also lingan me soor and my entire body aches. Only I know how much I suffer!"

"Yes, Nani," said IRB caressing her arm gently. "And what will you have for lunch today?"

"The grandchildren love tikki ain sambosa. You remember how you used to love sambosa too, when you were small? You would come and sit on my lap and lisp, "Nani, tamosa banao," so sweetly! And I would make them for you myself, whenever you came to stay with me. I had strength in those days. Well these children are like you. Today I will have just two tikkis or two sambosas and a plate of bhajiyas, with a little chattani and a small roti and a bowl of curd and rice. I'll call that kaamchor Shanti to warm tikki and 'tamosa' for you. She always disappears when I need her and pretends to be deaf."

"Nothing for us, Nani. But you must change your diet and …"

"No, no. I have too many problems already. How can I change? I will feel worse. Pet saaf kana tho ache."

"Nani you must have papaya and other fruits. Then your digestion will work."

"No, no. Papaya is too garam. It will bring heat in my body! Even in Sindh I did not like that fruit. Maybe in the evening I will feel better."

"How is that?" asked IRB.

"I have a chŭkri in my little silver glass. And then that chari Shanti will bring my chillum or I sometimes send her to get me a beedi from the paanwalla downstairs. It really helps my digestion. In Sindh, of course you don't remember, but my grandmother also used to have her **chūkrī** and hubble-bubble in the evenings. It takes away all the **vaī-baadī** from the body."

"Nani You have to control your food and you must exercise …!"

"Now Thadri is coming, and there is so much work. And we will be eating cold food. So I'll have only **lolas** and **kokī** and dahi vadas and mithais all prepared the previous day. All cold. We don't light the fires on Thadri as you know. I will be sending some Thadri prasad for your mother and for all of you also."

"Nani please don't eat **lolas** and **kokīs**", insisted IRB, "they are too heavy! I will send you some fresh fruit. Just eat that!"

"Arrey how can I live on that? As it is I have given up my non-veg. How I used to love my **teevan jo kando** and my **sayal pallo**. Oh how I wish I was back in Sindh to have it!"

"Nani, things change when we get older! You have to change too."

"Of course, I have changed. Our **teevan** in Sindh was so tender and juicy. And they used to cut it so nicely – all chops. Here I don't know what they do. It is so hard. I have changed. I don't eat it. And I don't eat chicken. Those kukurs eat rubbish. In Sindh where did we eat kukur? We ate **palla**. Only the servants ate chicken!"

"It is good that you are not eating mutton, but …"

Just then a little boy, came limping in.

"That little baby, see Mohan's son. He is not keeping well."

A two or may be three-year-old pale-looking boy was

waddling in on shaky spindly legs. Nani called out to him.

"Come, come, my Jaanu, come to Amma." Then she continued:

NANI IN HER GLORY DAYS IN KARACHI

"He is so pale. The doctor says he has less blood. Thullasim something. I don't know what that means. He says it is a Sindhi problem. Sindhi problem! God knows I never heard of this in Sindh. All these diseases are attacking us because of Partition. After Partition even your Nana became so ill."

"Nani this problem has nothing to do with Partition, it is thallasaemia, a condition in which ..."

"Now **pŭtt-a**, you can go. Spend good time with your bride. I am about to get my **ograï**. It is this Partition problem which gives me gas and sehko. I will rest a little."

And with that Nani once again called that '**mūee** Shanti' to pick up the child as he had fallen and started to cry.

Then she lay back on her pillow, dreaming of her happy days in Karachi.

12. A RICH LANGUAGE WITH NO TERRITORY IN INDIA

Vandana often asked me why Sindhi is written from right to left. And why we use the Arabic script to write it. She would watch with fascination when her grandparents read Sindhi books, and when her grandmother wrote the dhobi's account in Sindhi. Having grown up speaking Hindi at home and English in school, it took her some time to pronounce the implosives of her mother tongue: ba, da, ja, ga.

The language of Sindh was influenced, over the centuries, by not just the languages of its neighbouring territories but also by the languages spoken by its invaders, giving it some phonetic sounds and grammatical structures that have puzzled linguists.

These influences have also made it a very rich language which indicate the discerning levels of thought of its speakers. It is a language that gave rise to a powerful literature and philosophy from our spiritual seekers and poets such as Shah Abdul Latif Bhitai, Sachal Sarmast, Sami and others. More recently came Bedil, Bekas, Dalpat, Bewas and others, better known by their descriptive and poetic pen names rather than the ones they were given at birth. Our Sindhi **pahakas** are packed with folk wisdom and common sense. Some family favourites are:

daney daney tay mohir – every grain of food is engraved with the name of the eater (indicating a deep acceptance of destiny)

jahaan jeeyū, tahaan sikhū – learning continues, as long as one is alive

khūshee jairee khorak kohne, gam jairo marz kohne – there is no better nourishment than joy, no disease worse than worry

There are many more.

It's not just our expressions but our words that are colourful too! Here is an interesting example given by professor Popati Hiranandani:

A cow which has delivered a calf is referred to as **sooa**

A cow which does not want to give milk **khatar**

A cow which has stopped giving milk **phūndi**

A cow which has no horns **rodi**

A cow which has twisted horns **kūndhi**

This rich vocabulary reflects the language of a people who think clearly and understand detail and distinction. Our **prolis** (puzzles) too are so picturesque. One of my favourites is: **mūdis tangyo piyo ahey, zala paee ghūme**. The literal translation is that the husband is a stay-at-home, while his wife roams around. The answer to the puzzle: a lock and key!

How sad that our younger generation has lost this language.

Sindhi is an Indo-Aryan language with some relationship to the neighbouring Dardic (Kashmiri and Pashto), Iranian (Balochi) and Dravidian (Brohi) languages. Due to the Muslim influence since the eighth century AD, Sindhi vocabulary and grammar is saturated with Arabic and Persian elements. It includes several Perso-Arabic sounds not native to Indo-Aryan.

The annexation and the language

When the British conquered Sindh in 1843, there were a number of scripts in use, the most common being the Chaliha Akhari – a script of forty letters. Muslims did not give much priority to education, but they studied the Quran, and were familiar with the Arabic script. It was the British who declared Sindhi as the official language of the province. Sir Bartle Frere, the first Chief Commissioner of Sindh from 1850 to 1859, issued an order in 1851 requiring all officials and civil servants to pass an examination in the Sindhi language. Thus arose the need to settle a definite, distinctive and standard script of the Sindhi language. Devanagari script was considered, but it was just as foreign to the Sindhi Hindus as to the Sindhi Muslims. A committee of eight scholars – four Hindus and four Muslims – discussed the matter, and put together a script with fifty-two letters, an alphabet which was adopted in 1853.

In 1947, when our beleaguered community was compelled to leave Sindh, we naturally took our language with us. However, when the Indian Constitution was framed in 1950, it accepted fourteen Indian languages, and Sindhi was not one of them. This came as a shock to Sindhi writers and intellectuals! We had lost our land – and now we were going to lose our language too. It took a long legal battle before Sindhi

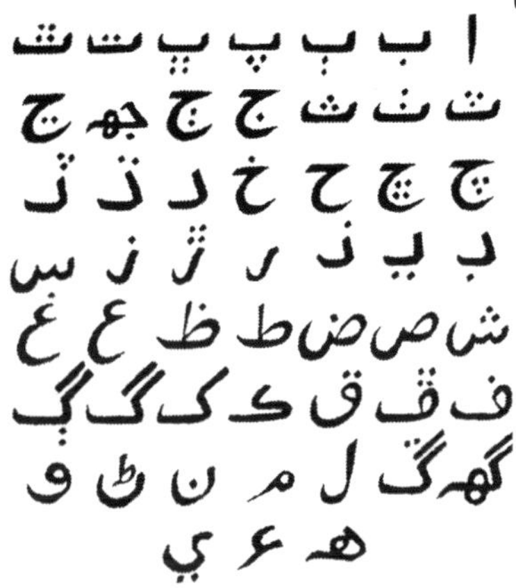

Alphabets of the Sindhi language
Image courtesy Lakhmi Khilani

was finally accepted as a language under Schedule VIII of the Constitution of the Republic of India on 10 August 1967 – giving Sindhi the distinction of being the only constitutionally recognized language in India without a territory.

In those twenty years, a generation of children had grown up without having learnt Sindhi. Moreover, in the turmoil following Partition, Sindhi parents did not see the benefit their children would gain from learning Sindhi: they wanted them to learn local languages so that they would integrate well in local communities and progress in their lives. The children, too, were happy enough learning the literature of other, more 'important' languages in school and college!

The controversy

In 1948, a controversy erupted over which script should be used for writing Sindhi; it was a controversy which would deal a further blow to the already weak propagation of Sindhi in India. Should Sindhi be written in the Arabic script or should it be written in the Devanagari script?

The campaign to change the script from Arabic to Devanagari was started by some of our own Sindhi patriots of the Indian National Congress, led by Jairamdas Daulatram Alimchandani, who after Partition would serve as Governor of Assam and then Union Minister of Food and Agriculture of the Government of India.

The pro-Devanagari faction held that the Arabic script was a 'Muslim script' of the Koran and had been imposed on unwilling Hindus by the British and the majority community of Sindh. Also, since the Indian National Congress wanted Hindi as the national language of Independent India, the Devanagari script was a suitable one, and claiming it as appropriate for Sindhi was an act of patriotism. But this struck another blow to the language of the already scattered community.

When the pro-Devanagari group passed a Resolution and informed the Government of India that the Sindhi Hindus in India had decided to change the script from Sindhi Arabic to Devanagari, the Sindhi academics, writers and intellectuals were taken by surprise as, according to Art 29(1) of the Constitution of India, the distinct script of the Sindhi language is the Arabic script and no other, and this is an absolute right conferred by this Article. They argued that each language has a genius of its own, which can only be expressed in its own language. Besides, the wealth of Sindhi literature, all of it written in Arabic Sindhi, would be lost to those who studied Devanagari Sindhi. "Can a language have a religion?" asked Madan Gopal angrily in his 1953 book *This Hindi and Dev Nagri.*

The matter came to Court. Ram Jethmalani, eminent laywer and politician, contested on behalf of the petitioners, and the equally competent Hotchand Advani appeared for the respondents. Justice KK Desai ruled on behalf of the petitioners, stating that:

> The students whose parents are Sindhis and whose language had been written in Arabic Sindhi script, are they not entitled to the same consideration and treatment as the other communities? ... Sindhis are entitled to equal treatment like other communities in the impartation of education in primary schools like Maharashtrians, Gujaratis, Tamils and Telugus. The treatment meted out to them in this changeover has been grossly discriminatory as is contended on behalf of the petitioners ... Under the circumstances, the petitioners are entitled to succeed.

Popati Hiranandani was loud in her support of the Arabic

script. She wrote bitterly in *Sindhis: The Scattered Treasure*:

> Firstly, our leaders made no attempt to save even a small part of Sindh for the Sindhi Hindus (unlike the leaders of Bengal and Punjab). Secondly, when the Constitution of India was being drafted and all the modern Indian languages were being listed in the Eighth Schedule, they made no effort to get the Sindhi language included in the Schedule which caused the Sindhis innumerable hardships for eighteen years till the Constitution was ultimately amended in 1968.

Today when so few of our youngsters know the Arabic script, it might just have been possible for them to learn Sindhi in the Devanagari script as many of our children are familiar with Hindi and the Devanagari script becomes easier with fewer alphabets.

THE TRAVESTY

The Sindhi language continues to flourish in Sindh, where it is spoken, read and written with love and respect. It is neither a national language nor an official language of Pakistan. In India, despite being one of the scheduled languages of our constitution, Sindhi is sadly a dying language.

13. A statue for Raja Dahir

the brave king of Sindh

One day, I happened to come across an article in the magazine *Aseen Sindhi*: "Sindhupati Samrat Dahirsen Smarak inaugurated". Intrigued, I read on:

> Ajmer situated in the heart of the desert state of Sindh, is home to many a religious monument ... it is home to the famous dargah of the Islamic faith and Pushkar, which is barely 6 miles away and one of the holiest places of worship of Hindus. Situated here in Ajmer is the recently inaugurated monument of Sindhupati Dahirsen, which has become one of the main attractions of this desert town.

When I spoke to Bhau Jairam Rupani, editor of *Aseen Sindhi*, he explained to me that Raja Dahirsen's empire had covered a large area which included Kachchh as well as towns of Rajasthan now on India's border, and that Ajmer was indeed at its heart.

I knew a little about Raja Dahirsen, the last Hindu ruler of Sindh, and was happy to read that the monument is designed to look like a fort and display glimpses of the history of Sindh. These include the ruins of the ancient civilization of Mohen jo daro and pictures of Jhulelal, Sant Kanwar Ram, Hemu Kalani and of course Raja Dahirsen.

Soon after this, I read another bit of interesting news. A political group in Pakistan too, wished to commemorate the memory of Raja Dahirsen with a statue, but was facing strong opposition! My curiosity roused, I started reading to try and find out more about Dahirsen and why his statue was controversial.

CHACHNAMA AS A SOURCE

I first turned to the *Chachnama*, ostensibly the oldest history of Sindh, looking for an answer. However, the ancient text seemed to have more questions than answers! I will mention just a few here:

- The original was an eighth century work in Arabic, which is lost.
- In the thirteenth century, Ali Kufi translated the Arabic into Persian, a better-known language at the time. He referred to his work as a **tarjūma** – translation.
- In 1900, the literary doyen and noted historian Mirza Kalich Beg, translated the Persian into English.

Having come down to us over centuries and through two translations, our Chachnama is not a work that was written in the eighth century or even the thirteenth century but a work that changed and evolved through the interpretations of those who wrote it, and in the context of the world view prevalent during their time.

RICHARD BURTON

I then looked up my copy of Richard Burton's *Sindh and the Races that Inhabit the Valley of the Indus* (1851). Burton – historian, explorer, scholar, soldier and diplomat – could not resist writing on every conceivable subject. And I was sure I would find something there. This is what he wrote:

> According to the Moslem historians, a dynasty of five Rahis, who had their capital at Alor, ruled the lovely land of Sindh in ease and prosperity for

> about 140 years. In the seventh century of our era, Rahi Sahasi the Second died, without children, and his queen, after causing the death of all the rightful heirs, bestowed it upon her paramour, one Chach, a priestly politician ... His reign lasted forty years, and on his death he was succeeded by their son Dahirsen.

With this peek into the history of Sindh, I was ready to garner more information about these rulers of our erstwhile homeland from other sources.

The Arab invasion

Unfortunately, not much has been written about Sindh, but certain facts stand out. The powerful kings of the Rai dynasty ruled Sindh for 137 years and in 622 AD, the fifth and last king died childless and with him came the demise of the Rai dynasty. His Brahman chief minister Chach seized power and also the love of the widowed Queen Suhandi, whom he married. She bore him two sons: Dharasiah and Dahirsen. Chach died after a rule of forty years. After his death, his brother Chander, a devout Buddhist, reigned

Relics of a Buddhist stupa at Mirpur Khas
from *Antiquities of Sindh* (1922) by Henry Cousens.

for seven years. Buddhism was a major religion of Sindh at the time as is evident from the many Buddhist relics in Sindh. When Chander died, Dahirsen became the ruler.

At this time, 'Sindh' was generally referred to as the valley of the Sindhu River, and covered a large territory which included Kandahar, Kashmir, Kanauj, Makran and more. The king of this region resided at Aror, the ancient capital near the site of which the modern towns of Sukkur-Rohri face each other across the Sindhu, with the fort of Bukkur on an island in between. Aror, we are told, was a town adorned with various kinds of royal buildings and villas, gardens, fountains, streams and meadows. It was a land of wealth and prosperity.

The glorious Sindhu river and the famed wealth of the region attracted invaders. Being in a strategic position, it was constantly under threat. Always prepared to ward off invaders, it produced brave and courageous martyrs and rulers who were constantly vigilant but are not remembered today.

THE BRAVE RAJA DAHIRSEN

Between 638 and 711 AD, the Arabs are said to have made fifteen attempts to invade Sindh, which were successfully rebuffed. On the sixteenth attempt, in the time that Al-Hajjaj ibn Yusuf was Governor of Iran, they were successful. Initially Caliph Walid had written to al-Hajjaj: "The affair will be a source of great anxiety and so we must put it off". But al-Hajjaj became adamant. He appointed the seventeen-year-old Muhammad bin Qasim as commander. As the story goes, Muhammad bin Qasim had his horses and camels clad in coats to look like lions. The Sindh army was taken by surprise, but they fought bravely. The Arabs floundered, and it appeared that they had fled, defeated. Then, suddenly, a fiery arrow hit Dahirsen, followed by a shower of more arrows. His men lost heart and the end came on 6 June 712. Dahir's beloved son Jaisiah too lost his life. The north Indian kingdom of Kanauj could have helped Dahirsen. But after the death of Harsha in 647, it was too weak to help even itself, much less others. Sindh fought and fell alone.

As soon as the news of Dahirsen's death reached his queen, she rose to the occasion to continue the battle, but when her troops deserted her, she committed sati. Her two daughters joined the ranks, but they were captured and brought to Muhammad bin Qasim, who handed them to the Caliph, his master, to please him.

When the Caliph questioned the weeping girls, they informed him that Muhammad bin Qasim had already defiled them. The Caliph was furious and ordered that bin Qasim should be brought to him stitched in the skin of an ox. By the time Muhammad bin Qasim was brought, he was dead. There are many versions of what happened next but it seems most likely that the Caliph handed over the girls to his troops for their merriment. Both girls are said to have committed suicide.

This briefly is the legend of the brave Dahirsen and his family.

Nationalism and anti-nationalism

Bias in the presentation of history is common, and doubly so in the case of the Chachnama written hundreds of years ago, and twice-translated, and coming to us not from the horse's mouth but the grapevine.

Nationalists in Pakistan portray Muhammad bin Qasim as a young hero who brings the teachings of the Prophet Mohammad into a pagan land and wages war against the ageing Dahirsen, a tyrannous Ravana-Kans type villain.

On the other hand, the Sindhi sub-Nationalists in Pakistan showcase Dahir from the other side of the spectrum; their Dahir is Ram, or Krishna. And Muhammad bin Qasim is the Ravana-Kans who routed and robbed Sindh of her treasures and spread a reign of terror among peace-loving people. Each side has it hardcore supporters.

So now the 'Dahirsen statue controversy' in Pakistan became clearer to me, and more so after I read about GM Syed, a prolific writer and politician; one who carried his searing regret for his initial support for the creation of Pakistan to the grave. He included Dahirsen as one of the champions of the Sindhi nation in his 1967 book *Sindh ja Surma* – The Heroes of Sindh – describing him as one of the five champions of the Sindhi nation who had been killed by Arab invaders. He protested against Muhammad Bin Qasim being projected as a hero by the Pakistan Government, which had named ports, roads, libraries and colleges after him, describing bin Qasim as an Arab tyrant who colonised Sindh, and condemned thousands to enforced slavery.

In 1972, Syed proposed the formation of an independent nation for the Sindhis under the name of Sindhudesh. He challenged the rulers and emerged as a controversial figure and in consequence suffered house arrest, imprisonment, and sufferance for nearly three decades in Pakistan, a political prisoner for the same duration as Nelson Mandela. In 1992, his house was declared a sub-jail; he died there, still under house arrest, in 1995.

Facing the bitter truth

G M Syed had been very much for Pakistan during the years leading up to Partition, and had been bitterly vocal against the Hindus. In November 1939, he was one of the political leaders who led a mob to forcibly occupy Masjid

Manzilgah, a group of buildings facing Sadh Belo, claiming that it had been a mosque during Akbar's reign. And he had loudly asserted, on the floor of the Sindh assembly, that the Hindus would be driven out of Sindh like the Jews from Germany.

Later, as stark realities began to show themselves, his volte face was severe. Syed went to the extent of saying that Pakistan was a folly and a crime, that refugees had ruined the country, that West Punjab had reduced Sindh to a colony, and that Pakistan would have to die for Sindh to live and breathe freely again. And he added:

> Why blame the Hindus for Muslim backwardness? Every morning when the Hindu child takes his bath and goes to school, the unwashed Muslim child is seen playing marbles in the dirty by-lane.

He reiterated, "The Sindhis weep for Imam Hussain and they weep for Raja Dahirsen." For Sindhis, the religion of a person does not come in the way of recognizing great souls and great heroes which is as it should be. He staunchly supported Dahirsen as a hero.

On his last visit to Delhi, in 1987, Syed's friend Anand Hingorani, a leading member of the Indian National Congress in Sindh and very close to Gandhi, said to him in good humour: "I have come to protest. You are responsible for our leaving Sindh! It was you who moved the resolution in favour of Partition in the Sindh Assembly."

Syed replied: "I plead guilty. But even a murderer gets only twenty years; I have already suffered for forty years."

A balanced view

Raja Dahirsen was indeed a hero. He worked hard to consolidate the territory around Sindh and to ward off innumerable invasions from the Arabs and others. He offered asylum to Imam Hussain, grandson of the prophet Mohammad, who was married to a Sindhi girl. He gave him every support and assistance, but Hussain was persecuted, and he was killed while he was on his way to Sindh.

So, should Pakistan erect a statue in memory of Raja Dahir? Perhaps, perhaps not. After Partition, statues in Pakistan were pulled down and defaced. But even if Pakistan does not believe in statues, the brave Raja Dahirsen must not be denied his due place in history! The past must not be ignored. I strongly recommend that a chapter titled Dahirsen and the history of Sindh should be included in the textbooks of both India and Pakistan.

14. The beheaded benefactor and other Bharvanis

While surfing the internet some time ago, I came across a headline in *Dawn* newspaper which read: *Karachi's Beheaded Benefactor.*

Under this headline appeared the picture of a statue: a dapper gentleman dressed in a fully European style suit, complete with bowtie and waistcoat. Except for one important detail: the statue stood headless! This gave me the shivers. But what made my hair really stand up was when I read on and realized that the "Harchand Rai Vishin Das" mentioned in the *Dawn* article was an illustrious family member, Seth Harchandrai Vishindas Bharvani (1862-1928). I began to wonder why his head had been lopped off. Surely not during his lifetime – wouldn't I have heard about this savagery from family members?

Journalist Akhtar Baloch explains in his article that this act of destruction took place some time after Partition, when Karachi "moved from religious plurality to extremism and intolerance". In spite of protests from the family over the last few decades, and their continuous pleas that the statue be repaired and restored, Seth Harchandrai's statue remains headless in a Karachi Municipal Corporation warehouse.

The first thing that a dictatorial government does when it comes to power is to destroy past history so that it can rewrite history and project itself as the epitome of all the progress that has ever happened in the country. In the novel *1984* by George Orwell, the totalitarian government of Oceania repeatedly announces, "increase in chocolate rations" and "innumerable victories". The Ministry of Records is busy destroying previous records and creating new records which will establish the new dictator as the Messiah of Mankind who increases chocolate rations and wins innumerable victories.

The act of desecrating the statue of a Hindu Sindhi who was recognized as the Father of Modern Karachi, by the newly-formed government of a country created by Partition, is an example of history being rewritten. Perhaps one day the statue will be given a new head and Modern Karachi will have a new father. Until then, I decided to continue reading and reviewing written sources within the family to learn more about IRB's illustrious forefathers.

I learnt that it was on his sixth death anniversary, at a well-attended program at the Karachi Municipal Corporation Building in 1934, that the statue of Seth Harchandrai Vishindas Bharvani was unveiled. Leading personalities paid homage to the services and hard work that he had put in at the KMC during the thirty-three years he had been associated with it. The statue, which was to be placed at the entrance of the majestic KMC building in his memory, had been planned after his death by then British Commissioner,

THE STATUE OF SETH HARCHANDRAI VISHINDAS BHARVANI OUTSIDE THE KARACHI MUNICIPAL CORPORATION BEFORE PARTITION

Karachi's Beheaded Benefactor: what happened to the statue after Partition.

Walter Frank Hudson, and a committee of leading citizens of Karachi. A moving speech was delivered at the unveiling by his nephew Hiralal Bharvani, a well-known academic and later principal of the DG National College in Hyderabad.

One of Karachi's city fathers

Seth Harchandrai's work with the KMC began in 1888, when he was just twenty-six, and he continued to be associated with it in various capacities – as a member on several committees, as legal adviser, and finally as elected President for ten years. It may be noted that, as Saaz Aggarwal observes in her book *The Amils of Sindh* (2019): "To be a member of the Hyderabad or Karachi Municipal Corporation in those days was a matter of high prestige, a recognition of mature authority and administrative competence, not at all the kind of sleazy opportunistic identity associated with a similar position in today's India."

Seth Harchandrai's first initiative started with making Karachi a healthy town. When the British took over Sindh, they had converted a part of Karachi into a military camp. The old town too continued to grow, becoming over-populated with insufficient sanitary arrangements. Seth Harchandrai began to institute better payment to sanitary workers, repair of roads, building of footpaths. Streets were given a facelift. He travelled to Calcutta and Bombay and later to London to study urban planning. The people of Karachi were happy with his work and named an important road after Seth Harchandrai. This was one of the many Karachi roads to be re-named after Partition. I think the current name is Siddiq Wahab Road.

A FAMILY TRADITION

Sindhis are known for their philanthropy, but not so much for their deep patriotism and community service, and it was with joy and pride that I found more and more examples of it in my family. One of the earliest recorded incidences was as far back as 1897, when Sindh was ravaged by plague. Seth Harchandrai and his family attended to the sick with free offers of food, medicine, clothing and care. His father, Seth Vishandas Nihalchand, one of the pioneers of the cotton ginning business in Sindh, a forest contractor, and owner of several rice-threshing factories and a fleet of boats, built a separate hospital to quarantine the infected patients. Seth Vishindas had also been a Councillor of the Karachi Municipality and in recognition of his services, which included the building of a library, a school and a rest house, he was honoured by the British in 1898 with the title of Rao Bahadur.

Sitting: Udhavdas Vishindas, Srichand Vishindas, Harchandrai Vishindas, Vishindas Nihalchand, Keshodas, Jethomal, Jashanmal Wasyomal, Jairamdas, Naomal

Standing: Gusain Dev, Devraj Dev, Devkishin Dev, Ghouse Dev. **Sitting on the floor**: Golu, Sukhdev Udhavdas, Aiel

From *Ratanjyot*

One of the most notable achievements of Seth Harchandrai during his tenure at the KMC, mentioned by historians and cited in Akhtar Baloch's article, was attending to the waterlogging in Karachi caused by the Lyari river. The Lyari flowed through the centre of the city, periodically overflowing and putting people living on its banks at risk. Mosquitoes and other creatures also caused disease and gave rise to unhealthy conditions. Seth Harchandrai consulted engineers and a bund was built to prevent flooding. A new locality came up on the old river bed and though many wanted it to be named after Seth Harchandrai, he refused, suggesting it be named Lee Quarters after the engineer whose work had led to its creation.

In 1921, Seth Harchandrai was elected to the Indian Legislative Council on a Sindh seat reserved for non-Muslims. Earlier he had been an elected member of the Bombay Council. Both these positions entailed regular travel to Delhi. He reluctantly stepped down from his position at the Karachi Municipal Corporation, and *The Daily Gazette* reported:

> We regret Seth Harchandrai has resigned. The Karachi Municipal Corporation will be lucky if it gets a President who has Seth Harchandrai's qualities of head and heart.

Committed to a Secular Nation

The politics of Sindh and the Indian Freedom struggle are both tied up with the life of Seth Harchandrai. The province that he was born in was largely tribal and almost fully agricultural. There were a few urban centres: Karachi, the capital, and the two major trading entrepots: Hyderabad and Shikarpur. The wealthy merchants in these cities were Hindu zamindars of the Bhaiband class, while the administration was largely made up of the Amils who had for generations served as clerks and munshis in the government, having educated themselves in the language of the ruling class, first Persian and then English.

Rao Bahadur Vishindas Nihalchand Bharvani
(1843-1929)

Writing in her book *Sindh Through the Centuries* (1994), the historian Dr Hamida Khuhro, former Minister of Education of Sindh, said:

> Sindh became politically conscious with the advent of Ghulam Muhammad Khan Bhurgri who returned to Sindh from England after completing his studies in 1908.
>
> Bhurgri's politics were on a level altogether more advanced and around him gathered a band of selfless nationalists who were interested in working for the masses. Among them were Jairam Daulatram, Shaikh Abdul Majid Sindhi, Shaikh Noor Mahammad and Seth Harchandrai Vishindas Bharvani.

In 1909, British parliament passed The Indian Councils Act 1909, also known as the Minto-Morley Reforms, which dismayed Indian nationalists. Firstly, it brought about a limited increase in the involvement of Indians in the governance of their country. Not only were the number of Indian representatives in the Council minimal, they were only allowed to give advice and not actively participate. Secondly, there was strong objection due to separate electorates based on religion. Seth Harchandrai, a liberal humanist, a Sufi and a Theosophist, could not accept the idea of separate electorates along religious and communal lines. Both Seth Harchandrai and Bhurgri fought for greater representation for 'Indians'. Both also protested against the unfair treatment and neglect of Sindh by the British Government.

Sindh, a remote part of the Presidency with its distinct culture and geography, was under the jurisdiction of a British Commissioner with limited powers and used at best as a recreation ground for officials who enjoyed shikar in winter before returning to Bombay. This had been the condition since 1847, when Sindh was included in the Bombay Presidency by Charles Napier. Even Sir Bartle Frere, Commissioner in Sindh (1847-1853) and recognized as one of the best administrators of Sindh, expressed his unhappiness with this arrangement.

Seth Harchandrai with Ghulam Muhammad Khan Bhurgri on a vist to Europe c1930s

Separation of Sindh from Bombay Presidency

If Sindh was separated from Bombay, it would have a government of its own, and its own specific needs could be addressed. Highlighting Sindh's distinctive and individual character, Seth Harchandrai argued at the Karachi session of the Congress in 1913, of which he was chairman of the reception committee[1], that the region deserved autonomy because it possessed "several geographical and ethnological characteristics of its own, which give it the hallmark of a self-contained, territorial unit[2]." Harchandrai, Bhurgri, and others sought the backing of the secular Indian National Congress for Sindh's provincial autonomy. However, the unity of opinion between Muslim and non-Muslim politicians dissolved after communal riots in Larkana (1927) and Sukkur (1930).

This period was one of increasing communal dissension, with a resurgence of Arya Samaj and Hindu purity, which groups of the majority religion found objectionable. 'Shudhi' and 'Anti-Shudhi' movements are recorded from the time, with meetings being held and leaflets issued to create awareness and collect funds to 'reconvert' the 'Sanjogi Shaikhs', Hindu converts to Islam in Sindh.

The 37th anniversary of the Arya Samaj was celebrated in Karachi and made the occasion of a big demonstration[3]. Arya Samaj Pandits from elsewhere attended and delivered speeches so strongly anti-Muslim in tone that an open rupture between the two communities was narrowly averted. The leaders of both sides, realizing that

1 *The Sindh Story* by KR Malkani (1984)
2 Seth Harchandrai Vishindas quoted in *Alhaj Mian Ahmad Shafi, Haji Sir Abdoola Haroon: A Biography* (Karachi: Begum Daulat Anwar Hidayatulla, 1942), p70
3 *History of Non-Co operation Movement in Sindh*,1919-1924 : Maharashtra State Records, Ed. by BG Kunte, 1977 p118-119

A reception for Mohandas Gandhi (seen in the centre, wearing a turban) on his 1916 visit to Karachi. Seth Harchandrai and Ghulam Ali Chagla are seated on either side.
Image courtesy Ratan Jyot

these events might lead to open rupture and regrettable incidents, met privately in the house of Harchandrai Vishindas, on 8 September 1923, to see if a compromise could be achieved. It was decided that both Shudhi and anti-Shudhi movements might continue, but indecent attacks on either religion should be avoided. Resolutions to this effect addressed to the press and the people were then adopted and a board of conciliation was established with G. M. Bhurgri as President, Harchandrai Vishindas, Haji Abdullah Haroon, Moulvi Mahomed Siddik (not Sadik) and Jamshed Mehta as Vice-Presidents, with Choithram, Kazi Abdul Rehman and Santdas Mangharam as Secretaries, the last named to also be Treasurer.

Despite much effort, matters gradually became worse.

The separation of Sindh was still necessary for administrative reasons – but the movement became highly politicized. And, by the time the province was separated, in 1936, both Harchandrai and Bhurgri were no more. The environment had become more significantly polarized.

Seth Harchandrai's last ride

Dyarchy, a system of dual government, had been introduced by the Government of India Act, 1919, with a promise that Indians would be allowed to participate more in the governing of their own country. A decade after the Act was introduced, it was reviewed by the Simon Commission. Indians now expected to be given more participation in the government of their own country. But the Simon Commission had no Indian members. Seven British Members of Parliament arrived in Delhi on 16 February 1928, and were greeted by protests. Black flags were raised with the slogan "Go back Simon!" throughout the country. The police resorted to lathi charges to suppress the movement. Even senior leaders like Jawaharlal Nehru were

Seth Harchandrai Vishindas Bharvani (1862-1928)

not spared. Lala Lajpat Rai, who was leading a demonstration, was brutally lathi-charged and died due to the injuries sustained.

As a prominent member of the Legislative Assembly from Sindh, Seth Harchandrai was needed in Delhi to vote on a resolution to boycott the Commission at the Central Assembly. Sadly, the sixty-six-year-old Seth Harchandrai was ill and in no condition to travel. Even so, Sarojini Naidu, 'The Nightingale of India', made a special trip to Karachi to urge him to attend as the support and backing of his large following were needed in Delhi. Lala Lajpat Rai too sent telegrams requesting him to come to Delhi. So, against the orders of his doctors, Seth Harchandrai left Karachi on 14 February 1928. His condition worsened on the train and he was advised to leave the train and get medical aid, but he continued on the journey. When he reached Delhi, he was carried in a wheelchair to the car waiting for him. He died on his way to the Assembly.

An eminent Elphinstonian, a lawyer, and a social reformer

Seth Harchandrai always remembered the happy years he spent in Bombay while he was a student at the Elphinstone College, from where he graduated in 1882 with History and Politics. He continued at the college and received his Law degree in 1885.

One of the teachers he would recall, during evenings with friends at the Karachi Club or the Bhaiband Club, was Professor William Wordsworth, grandson of the poet William Wordsworth. A popular teacher, Professor Wordsworth's classes were always well attended. He continued coming to college even when he later became Sheriff of Bombay. In those days, the college was at Byculla[4], opposite what was then known as Victoria Gardens.

Seth Harchandrai, an excellent raconteur, had a captivating smile and baritone voice, and was always the centre of a charmed circle and this included fellow students Gopal Krishna Gokhale, Shyamjee Krishna Varma, and PJ Padshah, national leaders and intellectuals, who distinguished themselves in public life in the years to come.

After a short stint in government service on his return to Karachi, Seth Harchandrai set up his own law firm in 1886 at Bunder Road. His eloquence and quick thinking earned him a successful practice. He was elected Honorary Secretary of the Karachi Bar Association, on its inception in 1890 and he held this office for thirty-eight years! Seven clerks of his law office became advocates. Jinnah, too, interned at Seth Harchandrai's office before moving to Bombay for better prospects.

---

4 *Dhondo Keshav Karve* by GL Chandavarkar, Publications Division Ministry of Information & Broadcasting New Delhi (1970) https://books.google.co.in/books?id=CKo-DwAAQBAJ&pg The pages are not numbered.

Besides being a person who was forward-looking and concerned about the status of women, Seth Harchandrai practiced what he preached. When he lost his wife at a young age, a number of proposals of eligible young women came to the family. But Seth Harchandrai chose to marry a young widow, Atori bai. Widow re-marriage was a controversial matter, and this step taken by the family was seen as an example and a step towards the upliftment of women's status.

When I went to Kachchh with my sister and some friends, we visited the Shyamjee Krishna Varma Memorial set up by the Gujarat government. The Memorial's objective is to pay tribute to the contribution of Shyamji Krishna Varma and also to educate the younger generation about those great Indians who sacrificed everything for the country's freedom and the fight against foreign rule. While walking through it, I could not help but think that today, if we had our own Sindh, we too could set up memorials for our Sindhi leaders and philanthropists who worked selflessly for the country they were born in. There were innumerable such Sindhis – among them Hemu Kalani, Acharya Kripalani, K R Malkani, his brother N R Malkani – and so many, many others.

Instead stateless, as we are, Seth Harchandrai stands headless in a warehouse in Karachi, whose municipal corporation he nurtured for thirty-three years.

THE REVERED COLLEGE PROFESSOR PRINCIPAL HIRALAL SRICHAND BHARVANI

In one of his earliest letters to me (yes, we did write letters in those days ... nice long ones) soon after my marriage, when I had settled in Bombay, my father wrote: "Why don't you register for a PhD degree, since you have topped the MA English examination of Calcutta University and been offered a University Grant?"

Calcutta had once been the capital of the British Empire, and Calcutta University was established with the best of resources. On the fertile soil of Bengal, a state known for its intellectual and creative fabric, it flourished and, in the 1960s, even several years after Independence, it was one of the country's most respected universities.

I didn't jump at the suggestion. It was just a few months into my marriage and I was still trying to get used to a large joint family, to a new city, and to a brand new husband whom I had met just once before the marriage ceremony. I put the suggestion on the backburner and didn't think too much about it. There were so many more exciting things happening in my new life!

But very soon I received another missile enclosed with my father's letter: "You will find enclosed herein the enquiry letter from Calcutta University asking whether you plan to register for a PhD degree and avail of the University Grant or whether it should be allotted to the next suitable candidate." My father of course had included his own priceless suggestion: "Why don't you make a start? Think of a subject. Well begun is half done." My father loved his old proverbs, both English and Sindhi, and there was always one on the tip of his tongue for every occasion. When he needed my mother to darn his socks, he would remind her: "A stitch in time saves nine". And when my family was going through a tumultuous time in Bombay, he wrote to IRB: "Every cloud has a silver lining. This too will pass." In difficult times, I remember him and find these old proverbs comforting.

The latest epistle stimulated me, as I had begun to tire of 'all play and no work'. As a child of refugee parents, I had seen my father work hard during my school and college days to provide us four siblings with the best of everything. I decided to discuss the PhD registration subject with my father-in-law and of course IRB. I was surprised at their immediate reaction: "Go ahead," they both said happily, ignoring the fact that I and not they would be the sacrificial lamb!

At Elphinstone College

I stood there, fascinated, staring at the most magnificent Victorian architecture that Bombay could boast of. I had been informed by my Calcutta University professors that Elphinstone College was rated as the best in Asia. This made me nervous and a little overwhelmed as I headed towards its hallowed precincts.

The peon at the gate told me that the Principal's office was on the first floor. I ascended the stately broad staircase but not before I had taken a peek at the alcoves in the quadrangle where I could see small groups of students sitting, leaning leisurely against the solid stone walls, reading or writing or chatting, totally engrossed in whatever they were doing.

Outside the Principal's office, there stood a stately-looking turbaned durwan in white uniform and a broad sash around his waist. He handed me a chit to write my name on. Within a few minutes I was led through a door with Principal Bannerjee's name on it.

I remember my first impression of Principal Bannerjee so well. A small, almost frail-looking bespectacled man in charge of India's most renowned and prestigious college!

I entered and seated myself on one of the heavy mahogany Victorian chairs in the room, wondering whether I should introduce myself as a student from Calcutta University and maybe speak in Bengali (Bannerjee being a common Bengali surname). Glancing at the card which Aadam had handed to him, Principal Bannerjee looked up from behind his steel-rimmed spectacles and spoke to me in pristine Oxford-English: "Shakuntala Bharvani? Any relative of Principal Hiralal Bharvani?"

Being very new to the Bharvani family and my new name, I was not sure. But I reckoned that all Sindhis were connected. So I nodded my head.

His eyes twinkled. His smile became warmer and he said, "I became acquainted with Hiralal as we sailed to England together. I was on my way to Oxford and he was going to Cambridge. We spent a lot of time together on that trip. A fine man! He bore his learning lightly on his shoulders!"

After that introductory meeting, I met Banner (as we referred to him at Elphie) quite often. On another occasion, he mentioned that Hiralal was President of the Indian Majlis at Cambridge, and they had kept in touch. He also remembered that Hiralal had passed the English Tripos (Honours) with French and Italian. One day, he asked about our relationship. By then I was able to tell him that he was my husband's uncle and, coming from a large Sindhi joint family, the relationship was very close. In fact IRB's library consisted of several books which he had inherited from his uncle Hiralal!

I later learnt that Principal Bannerjee's area of specialization was language studies, which I did not plan to research on. He was subsequently appointed Head of the English Department of Bombay University, with an office at Club House, Churchgate. Still undecided about whether to register for a PhD degree and confused about which topic to select for my research work, I visited Elphie again. This time I found Kamal Wood in the Principal's chair.

Mrs Wood was a petite delicate-looking Parsi lady always attired in beautifully starched cotton sarees. I learnt later that the delicate look was deceptive: during the Quit India movement, the Oxford-accented voice on the Congress Radio was that of Koomie Dastoor. Being a government employee (Elphinstone is a government college), her identity remained undisclosed except amidst the inner circle. She also had some links with Indira Gandhi, as they had been friends at Oxford.

At Mrs Wood's suggestion, I decided to work on the stream-of-consciousness novel which seemed to suit my temperament. I considered myself lucky to have the first lady Principal of Elphinstone College as my PhD supervisor.

After Banner's affectionate enquiries about Hiralal, I wanted to know a little more about my family. We had two books at home: *Ratan Jyot*, written in Sindhi about the illustrious Bharvani family, and another titled Seth *Harchandrai Vishindas Bharvani: Father of Modern Karachi,* compiled by Khadim Hussain Soomro, a translation which I was able to read. Unfortunately, I could not read the former.

Hiralal was the nephew of Seth Harchandrai, eminent President of the Karachi Municipal Corporation and the first Hindu Member of the Legislative Assembly from Sindh. He was educated at the NJV High School and DJ Sind College, Karachi. His academic career was brilliant, and he was appointed Professor of English at Sindh National College, Hyderabad, in 1925 at the young age of twenty-one – probably the youngest professor in India.

While at Cambridge, he had been called to the Bar from Lincolns' Inn and for a brief period after his return he joined his uncle's legal firm, Harchandrai and Company, as an advocate in 1931. But his real calling was teaching, and he rejoined Sindh National College as senior Professor of English and French. In 1938 he was appointed Principal – it had been renamed Dayaram Gidumal National College in 1932 – and he continued in that position until Partition took place and the Sindhis were forced to leave.

It was always academia that attracted Hiralal, and teaching gave him the time and flexibility to indulge in his varied interests. He travelled extensively, mailing postcards to family members from various museums and art galleries he visited around the world.

I was curious to know why Hiralal never married. He was most eligible: wealthy, educated, highly-regarded, and belonging to the top rung of the Bhaiband landed gentry of Sindh. He was a Rotarian and International District Governor of Rotary (1945-46), a Freemason, a Theosophist, a member of the Dialdas and Bhaiband Clubs of

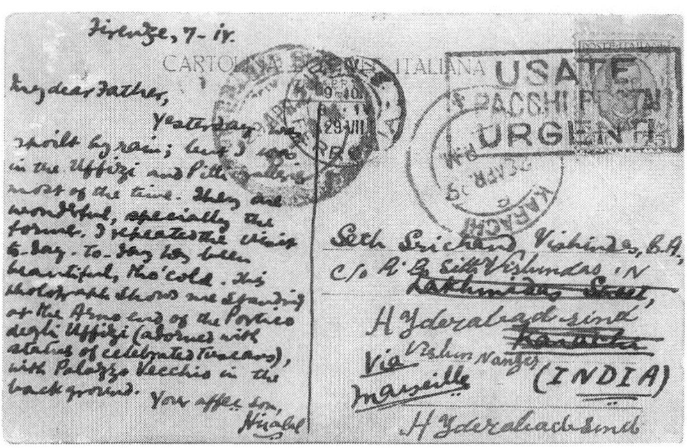
Firenze, 7-iv.

My dear Father,

Yesterday was spoilt by rain; but I was in the Uffizi and Pitti gallery most of the time. They are wonderful, especially the former. I repeated the visit to-day. To-day has been beautiful, tho' cold. This photograph shows me standing at the Arno end of the Portico degli Uffizi (adorned with statues of celebrated Tuscans), with Palazzo Vecchio in the background.

Your affec. son,
Hiralal

CARTOLINA POSTALE ITALIANA

USATE I PACCHI POSTALI URGENTI

KARACHI

Seth Srichand Vishindas, B.A.,
c/o R. B. Seth Vishindas N
~~Lakhmidas Street~~,
Hyderabad-Sind
~~Karachi~~
Via Marseille
(INDIA)
Hyderabad Sind

A postcard with young Hiralal's photo, written to his father from Florence in April 1929
Image courtesy Anil Bharwani

Hyderabad, and Karachi Club. Surely every elderly relative and acquaintance with an eligible daughter or niece must have had an eye on this eligible bachelor! There are many romantic and mysterious stories surrounding this young and sensitive genius, but the most poignant description I found was in the work of Popati Hiranandani:

> Mr Bharvani had not married. He spent his salary in granting student scholarships, and buying books and liquor. He had studied in England and, having surpassed his British classmates, had stood first in

> English Literature. But he was an unsuccessful man in his personal life. He had been in love with a girl in Hyderabad. As mentioned earlier, the Amils from Hyderabad never allowed their girls to fall in love. The girl's parents told Mr Bharvani, "We will give our girl to you after you complete your studies in England!" Soon after he left, they got her married to someone in Calcutta. Through business-related enmity, the girl's husband was killed, and she became the mother of his 'posthumous' son. Upon returning from England, Professor Bharvani realised that he had been beguiled. Despite this perfidy, he was still willing to marry the girl and adopt her son, but the girl's parents did not allow that to happen. He sacrificed his life in the name of love! His nights were devoted to music, wine, and study. He would listen to Sindhi songs from his servant, Morai, all through the night, drink wine and wake up as the spirit of Shakespeare in the morning ... Yet a beam of brilliance and intelligence would circle around the personality of this tall compassionate man when he entered the classroom in his black gown. I believe that no one, having heard Professor Bharvani's lectures even once, can forget him for the rest of his or her life.
>
> *Excerpted from* The pages of my life *OUP (2010) by Popati Hiranandani translated from Sindhi by Jyoti Panjwani, p54*

Family members believe that Hiralal did fall madly in love. But there were differences in family background, and disapproval from Bharvani family elders. Parents of his heartthrob hastily married her off to someone else before a scandal erupted and her reputation lost its virgin sheen. And then Hiralal's life followed the same style as the woe-begone lover Devdas.

Another story states that he fell in love with an Amil girl

whose lifelong ambition was to become an actress. The aristocratic Bhaiband Seth family did not approve of a girl from the salaried-Amil background. And to add fuel to fire: one on the verge of acting in a film! Acting was still not considered a suitable profession for a girl, eight or nine

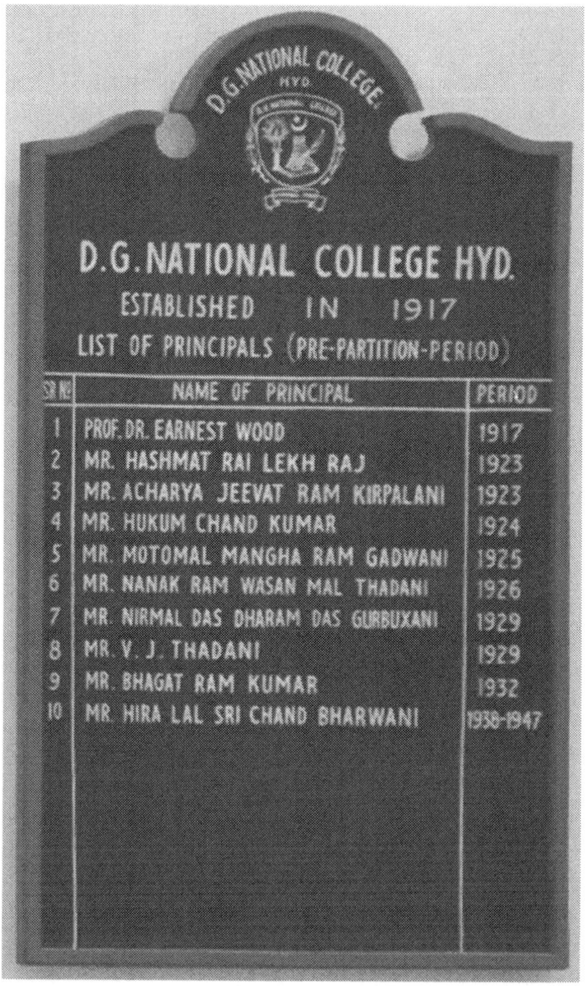

Principals of DG National College, Hyderabad, Sindh
Collection of Saaz Aggarwal

decades ago, as it entailed romping around trees and falling into the arms of strange men!

Principal Hiralal Srichand Bharvani
(1905-1949)

During his tenure at DG National College, the number of students at the college rose from three hundred to more than six hundred. But when Partition took place with the exodus of Hindus, just a handful of students remained.

Heartbroken as he was, Hiralal fell prey to a lingering illness soon after he left Sindh. He died in Delhi in 1949, when he was only forty-four. Suraj Prakash, son of Seth Harchandrai, cared for him in his last days, and performed his cremation on the banks of River Jamuna, later immersing his mortal remains in the River Ganga at Haridwar.

Seth Sukhdev Udhavdas Bharvani

Shortly after IRB and I got married, my father-in-law's oldest brother, Seth Sukhdev, who had stayed on in Karachi and never relocated to India, came to stay with us in Bombay for a few days to have a health check-up.

I had always wanted to visit Karachi, so I was quite excited. Both my brothers had been born in Karachi and my parents too had spent time there. I had heard about the city originally being a fort with two gates, the gate which faced the sea was called 'kharodar' as its water was salty, while near the other gate, named 'mithodar', stood a well with cool sweet water. It sounded like a miracle of nature! Then sundry relatives had also spoken of the historic Frere Hall, with the landmark Masonic Hall and the Sind Club in its vicinity, the NJV High School (where almost every member of the family seemed to have studied), and the Empress market named after Queen Victoria where you could shop for almost anything. And of course the Karachi Municipal Corporation where IRB's illustrious ancestor Seth Harchandrai had served the city in several capacities for thirty-three long years and where his statue had stood before it was desecrated and confined to a warehouse.

Now Burra Baba, as we called him, was coming to stay with us, and I would have the opportunity to learn a little more about Karachi. Perhaps a day would come when I would also visit the city and see the ancestral home there, and then travel on to Hyderabad to see the family's old ginning factory and other properties.

Burra Baba was almost twenty years older than my father-in-law, and he was a father figure to him, as their father Seth Udhavdas had passed away at a young age. We prepared for his arrival with care, and IRB scheduled Burra Baba's medical appointments two days after his arrival, so as to give him time to rest and recover after his journey. Imagine our surprise when the day after his arrival, the stately old gentleman announced to IRB that he wanted to visit Morarji Desai!

"Why?" I asked IRB, "Why does Burra Baba want to meet our deputy Prime Minister? He stays in Delhi and even if he is likely to visit Bombay while Burra Baba is here, surely he cannot just walk into his meeting room and say, "Ok Morarjibhai, I'm here to have lunch with you!"

IRB laughed, "Burra Baba is capable of doing just that!"

Dissatisfied with IRB's jocular reaction, I carried on in my best professorial voice, "And please remember Morarji Desai is an ascetic. He is a Gandhian. He eats simple food. And he drinks only urine-cola. "

"Yes!" said IRB, still highly amused, "but you must know Morarjibhai and Burra Baba are good friends. They spent days and nights together in the same cell in Nasik Prison and worked together in the days of our freedom movement. Anyway, I have to first find out if our Deputy PM is likely to visit Bombay, and then schedule a meeting."

SETH SUKHDEV UDHAVDAS BHARVANI (1896-1986)
IMAGE COURTESY HIS GRANDSON ANIL BHARWANI

Seth Sukhdev standing next to future Indian Prime Minister Jawaharlal Nehru, Karachi c1940s

It was then that I learnt that Seth Sukhdev had been jailed during India's struggle for Independence against the British not once but three times – in 1930, in 1932 and again in 1942.

It so happened that Burra Baba's Morarjibhai was indeed coming to Bombay and a meeting could be arranged! However, it was not destined. No sooner did the Deputy PM arrive than riots broke out in Bombay. Bal Thackeray had declared that no New Delhi leaders would be allowed to enter the city of Bombay if the central government did not cede the Marathi-speaking districts of Karnataka to Maharashtra. This was the beginning of Balasaheb Thackeray's political career and the protest he staged turned into a battle-scene when Morarji Desai arrived. Thackeray and other Shiv Sena leaders were arrested, and the Sena activists responded with an angry rampage, torching shops and buses, and attacking police stations. Several people were killed when Morarji Desai ordered firing to quell the crowds. Under these circumstances there was no question of Burra Baba meeting Morarji Bhai, much to his disappointment.

A leader of India's struggle for independence

Seth Sukhdev's active participation in India's freedom struggle began in 1921, when the Swadeshi movement was announced. He was twenty-five years old. It was a time when volunteers across India were going from house to house, collecting clothes made of foreign material. These would be thrown into a community bonfire and burnt. I had read an essay at school about how Indira Gandhi too as a child had thrown her foreign toys and dolls into such a bonfire. Burning foreign goods and pledging to use only

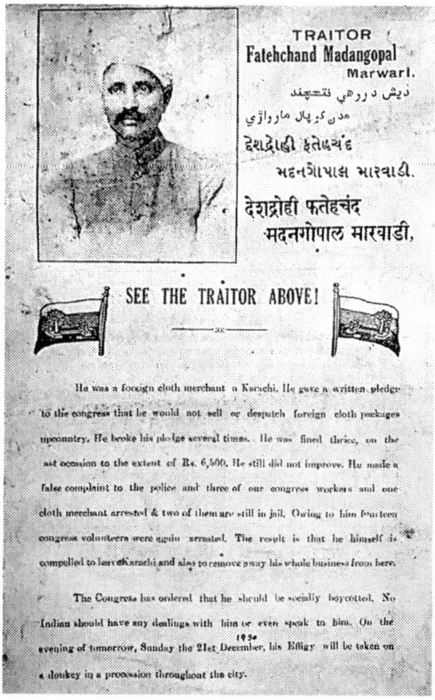

The poster condemning a traitor
Image courtesy Anil Bharwani

those made locally was a way to bring national pride to the people as well as to destroy the revenue of the colonial government.

Sukhdev was soon appointed secretary of the Foreign Cloth Boycott Committee as he was able to unite the businessmen of Karachi, particularly the cloth merchants. Nobody could buy or sell foreign clothes; anyone who did so would be fined. An affluent cloth merchant, Fatehchand Madan Gopal, continued trading in British fabrics. He was not only fined, but his effigy was taken out in a procession on donkeys, and burnt in a public place. I had heard about this incident from relatives and friends who had lived through this period. One of them even showed me a clipping with a photo which had appeared in *The Illustrated London News*.

Seth Sukhdev played an active part in the Satyagraha activities of 1930 and 1932. In August 1942, Gandhi announced Quit India and was arrested soon after. Other leaders of the Indian National Congress were also arrested, and the jails began to fill. In protest, Seth Sukhdev resigned as Trustee from the Karachi Port Trust. He was taken security prisoner on 21st October, and was eventually released from Sukkur Special Prison on 25 June

1943. I realized with a feeling of pride that this was the very place where Hemu Kalani, our Sindhi martyr, had been imprisoned, and his hanging had taken place during this period.

A LEADER OF THE HINDUS WHO REMAINED IN PAKISTAN

After Partition took place, events transpired which made it clear that Hindus were unsafe in Pakistan, and they began to flee. The newly-formed government of Pakistan tried to hold back people working in the 'essential services', the cleaning and sanitization workers of Karachi, as the city would collapse without them. Despite the fact that he himself had decided to stay on, Seth Sukhdev stood up for their rights and helped them with their paperwork and documentation. He believed that those who wished to leave should be free to make their own decisions. When GM Syed said to him, "Sukhdev, you have stayed on here and are seeing your Hindus brethren off as they leave the country. While I am here to welcome the Muhajirs," Sukhdev, not one to mince words, promptly replied, "Yes, my friend, and you are going to regret their arrival!" Unrest, looting and bloodshed followed, as the Muhajirs forcefully evicted the local Hindus from their homes. They did not hesitate to resort to shooting and using knives. A majority of the Muslim refugees who came to Sindh wanted to be rehabilitated in cities. "The population of Karachi," recorded Sri Prakasa, India's first High Commissioner to Pakistan, "rose from nine lakhs to fifteen. This sudden overcrowding created many problems."

The newly-formed government of Pakistan set up an official body to manage 'Evacuee Property'. Its primary objective appears to have been the acquisition of all properties that belonged to non-Muslims. Seth Sukhdev staunchly opposed the Evacuee Property Bill, holding that compensation should be considered before the government claimed the properties of people who had fled in fear but still legally owned them. He referred to the then Minister of Rehabilitation as a 'human octopus' and spoke out bitterly against the Government's tactics. Newspapers of the time reported these activities under the following headings: Seth Sukhdev puts forth Minorities' Grievances; Calls for Immediate Restoration of Properties and Temples to Non-Evacuee Hindus; Seth Sukhdev Supports Joint Electorate for Hindus; Seth Sukhdev Opposes Evacuee Property new bill, and others.

Prior to Partition and the installation of the new government, Seth Sukhdev had been Chairman and Director of Karachi Hindu Cooperative Bank (1937-39), Chairman of Karachi Cotton Association, Member of Senate of Karachi University, and several other prestigious positions. But the office he held closest to his heart was his presidentship of the Karachi Hindu Panchayat, the central organization of 20,000 Hindus and Harijans of Karachi. After Partition he was a member of the Constituent Assembly of Pakistan and its Standing Advisory Committee. Many Hindus did not agree with his policies, but they all recognized him as their leader and for them his word was law as they had utmost confidence in his integrity.

An expert in Labour Law Policy of the Sindh region, Seth Sukhdev was deputed to represent Pakistan in a conference on International Labour Organization in New Delhi, 1949.

An article titled *Leader of Sindhi Hindus* by Sarat Narasimhan, published in 1953 and now in our family album reads:

> Seth Sukhdeva Udhavdas is suave, simple and sober. He is no orator like silver-tongued Shaheed Suharwardy. But he can speak and speak forcibly.

> Modest, reserved and publicity shy, Sukhdeva is astute. Some call him foxy. He is certainly shrewd. Behind his bland, urbane exterior operates a subtle and highly resourceful mind. When ruffled he can be peppery. Then his black-white moustache bristles... Seth is a Pakistani first, a Hindu next... many Hindu leaders migrated to India, but Seth remained firm...

In 1965, when war erupted suddenly between India and Pakistan, Hindus who had come from India to visit their relatives and see their erstwhile homes in Pakistan were stranded. They could not leave, and lived in fear as Hindus were now all under suspicion. Seth Sukhdev sent out a message requesting funds for the temple trust, and these funds were used to house Hindus in safety and togetherness in the Swami Narayan Temple. He also organized home food to be delivered to them until their departure back home to India could be arranged.

I still remember that day, when Burra Baba entered our home, and we had all lined up near the entrance waiting to welcome him. I had stood all ready to bend down and touch his feet. But as he walked in, in his traditional khadi kurta and Nehru cap, and raised his hand in blessing to the whole family, I immediately understood that just like my father-in-law, Burra Baba did not believe in the ritual of touching feet.

15. Aapka desh kahan hai?

I was sitting with a friend while on a vacation to Kolkata, when her aged mother – a respectable and lovely-looking lady – came and joined us for a cup of tea. Her maid followed, with a plateful of peppered white dhoklas and methi nu thepla, and I was offered some. My friend's mother had arrived that morning from Ahmedabad, where she was visiting extended family, who had packed these local goodies for her to take to Calcutta. She complimented me on the South Indian kanjeevaram saree I was wearing, and then asked:

"Aapka desh kahan hai?" *Where is your country?*

I was taken aback by the question. Before I could reply, she said:

"Hum to Gujarat har saal jatay hain. Aap apne desh jatay hain kya?" *We go to Gujarat every year. Do you visit your hometown too?*

I was caught in a dilemma and, on the spur of the moment, replied:

"Hum Bombay mein rehtay hain." *We live in Bombay.*

She seemed satisfied. And, thankfully for me, did not pursue the subject.

This question, which arises periodically in the course of normal social interaction in our diverse land, haunted me for a while. I have always considered myself lucky to belong to a community which has the best doctors, the best hospitals, the top colleges, the most successful lawyers and even real estate developers. Whenever I travel, in India or abroad, I find my hospitable and friendly Sindhi brethren scattered everywhere.

I recently attended the wedding of my Sindhi nephew in Pune. He had met his wife-to-be in London. The girl informed me that she had been raised in Sri Lanka and that there were multitudes of Sindhis in Sri Lanka! They had active social organizations and met regularly to celebrate Sindhi festivals, during which they even sang Sindhi *ladas* together. They had also assimilated the culture of their adopted homeland: at the wedding, members of the bride's entourage were observed chatting away unconcernedly with each other in Sinhala, and dancing to the latest hits from Sri Lanka!

In Calcutta, my 'native' city, where my parents migrated after Partition, my father had been president of the Sindhi Social Centre which organized picnics, variety programs and festivals for members of the community so that we bonded and remained in touch. The highlight of these activities was Guru Nanak's birthday, which marked a festive period of five days. Punjabis joined in too, and we met morning and evening and enjoyed langar – communal meals – together. Cheti Chand, the Sindhi New Year, was another festival which the Sindhi families of Calcutta celebrated together. My community had made a comfortable niche for itself but the yearning for the lost homeland remained strong. And this yearning grew stronger with the passage of time.

The stringent visa regulations between India and Pakistan make it impossible to enter Sindh, but I was determined to visit the land of my ancestors one day, by hook or by crook! In 2019, I had the opportunity to view it from a distance, if not actually visit, along with my sister and some friends. From Bombay we travelled to Bhuj, the administrative capital of Kachchh district, by train, embarking at the Bhuj Railway station. It was an exciting moment, a first step in the journey to take a peek into our lost homeland.

On a visit to Amritsar some years previously, I had viewed the ceremonial closing of the gates at the Wagah border. It was by no means a glimpse into Sindh: the pomp and splendour and military pyrotechnics were merely reminiscent of Army Day celebrations, when the armed forces in full regalia march through cantonment areas. Bhuj had something quite different in store. We checked into the Tent City at Dhordo, and headed for the white desert.

The Rann

The white Rann of Kachchh is a great salt desert that lies between Gujarat in India and Sindh in Pakistan. We speak about the seven wonders of the world, but this Rann is not listed among them. When I beheld it, however, I felt there was no natural wonder greater than this. I had had a similar experience at Niagara Falls, the memory of which still sends a thrill down my spine and reminds me of the glory of God. There was no melody of rolling waters at the Rann of Kachchh, only salty, silvery sand. But the sight of this too was a wonder of God's heavenly creation. And it was only this Rann, about 7500 kilometres in area, that separated us that day from Sindh! Its beauty fascinated us, and we went to see it by day and then again at night, when the sight of it in moonlight struck me once more as a truly religious experience. I picked up a fistful of salty sand and later immersed it in half a cup of water. A few particles of sand sank to the bottom and the rest dissolved. When I tasted the clear liquid, its salt permeating my tastebuds, the same salt my ancestors savoured in Sindh, I was filled with emotion. There was an abundance of salt at my feet just waiting to be picked up.

After short visits to the major tourist sites in the area – a beach at Mandvi, a major seaport, the palace of the Maharao of Kachchh, and the Shyamji Krishna Varma Memorial Museum, we came to Kalo Dungar. This was another experience.

Kalo Dungar – the black hill – is the highest point in Kachchh, Gujarat, at 462m (1,516 ft), and famous for the 400-year-old Dattatreya temple situated on its highest peak. Due to its magnetic properties, we experienced the scientific anomaly of our vehicle defying gravity and rolling up the slope.

From Kalo Dungar, we had a glimpse of our Sindh. We couldn't see very much but the feeling of proximity to our original homeland was an emotional one.

Narayan Sarovar and Lakhpat

From Bhuj, we proceeded to Narayansar and Lakhpat, the places I was anxiously waiting to visit. I was specially inspired to take this trip by two of my friends who had told me so much about Kachcch: Dr Subhadra Anand and Aruna Jagtiani both connected in different ways to this region.

Aruna Jagtiani is the daughter of Pratap Dialdas Nanwani, a heroic Sindhworki with business in several countries of the world, and one who contributed generously, in innumerable ways, to the struggle for freedom against British rule. After Partition, his efforts were focussed on rehabilitating his community, displaced from their ancestral homeland. He was able to convince Gandhi to approach the Maharao of Kachchh to provide a place in his kingdom where a new Sindh could be built, Kachchh having historic links with Sindh and being geographically, culturally and linguistically akin to it. The Maharao generously donated

Bhai Pratap welcomes Indian Prime Minister Jawaharlal Nehru to the inauguration of Gandhidham
Image gourtesy Aruna Jagtiani

a part of his kingdom to set up a township for Sindhis, where Bhai Pratap, as he was respectfully known, initiated the founding Gandhidham and Adipur. He also identified a creek in the kingdom which, knowing the value of ports to a country's economy, he began to develop into a port.

Initially, Gandhidham and Adipur remained uninhabited and barren wastelands but over time and with focussed planning and efforts, they grew to be busy cities, commercially successful and centres of education for the community. Today, Kandla hosts one of the major ports of India, and land prices in the vicinity compare favourably with those in the big cities of India.

Jhulelal Tirathdham

Dr Subhadra Anand is an enterprising person best known for her seminal work, *National Integration of Sindhis* (1996), which formed the core of her PhD thesis. After working in academia right through her career, she retired as Principal of National College, Bombay. She then had a long stint in the field of social welfare, after which she took up a new and ambitious project: to establish a large cultural centre for Sindhis in the name of our 'homeless' community's most prominent religious icon, Jhulelal.

The land for the centre, a large expanse close to the Kori Creek at Lakhpat, was suggested by Madhav Joshi, a Partition refugee from Karachi now living in Narayansar.

The culture of the people of Kachchh is similar to that of the Sindhis, and Kachchhis too worship Daryalal. Lakhpat was once a part of Sindh, with the Sindhu river ending here before the earthquake of 1819 blocked it. It is the last village before the Indo-Pak border and stands perched on the edge of the Indus, which manifests here as the Kori Creek. With the Pakistan border just 40km from here, military posts along the creek keep a round-the-clock vigil.

Subhadra and a few other like-minded people set up the Jhulelal Dham Trust in 2007. As the project gathered momentum, they met Narendra Modi, Chief Minister of Gujarat, to share their vision and seek the necessary permissions. They hardly needed to explain to him how their project would contribute to the tourism and development of his state. The future Prime Minister of India responded with enthusiasm: "Your dream is my dream!" after which he sanctioned 73 acres of land to the project.

The members of the Jhulelal Dham Trust have envisioned not just a temple but also auditoriums and seminar halls, a museum, conference rooms, restaurants, high-quality accommodation for visitors, and these will make the complex self-sustaining. If you would like information or wish to contribute, please email info@jhulelaltirathdham.com.

Jhulelal Mandir

Jhulelal Mandir overlooks Narayan Sarovar, one of the holiest lakes of Hinduism, which include Mansarovar in Tibet, Pampa near Hampi in Karnataka, and Pushkar in Rajasthan. The earth around Narayan Sarovar is considered to be so sacred that one chant of 'OM' here has the power of 108 chants! It is believed that when severe drought affected the area, the celestial being Lord Narayan, an incarnation of Lord Vishnu, appeared in answer to the prayers of the sages. He touched the earth with his toe, at which water poured forth and a lake was formed. The lakes in this area are considered holy and, unlike water bodies around India, these are kept spotlessly clean by having established the belief that anyone defiling the waters would be cursed.

There is an ancient Shiva temple at Koteshwar, where the earth meets the sea. The story of Koteshwar begins with Ravana, who won a boon from Lord Shiva for an outstanding display of piety. This boon was the gift of a Shivalinga, an emblem of generative power, which had great spiritual energy. But Ravana, in his arrogant haste, accidentally dropped it and it fell to the earth at Koteshwar. To punish Ravana for his carelessness, the linga turned into a thousand identical copies! Unable to distinguish the original, Ravana grabbed one and departed, leaving the original one at Koteshwar.

Lakhpat is also the site of Gurdwara Pehli Patshahi, the Gurdwara of the first master, named to commemorate the numerous visits of Guru Nanak in the course of his travels. The Gurdwara's large showcase displays numerous relics, including the charan paduka (wooden footwear) believed to have been worn by him.

The glowing lights of Karachi were clearly visible from

the beach at Koteshwar, just about 100metres away, and the sea forms a perfect backdrop to Lord Jhulelal, who is believed to have emerged from it to protect us from the tyranny of conversion.

Visiting the Rann of Kachcch, walking around Lakhpat and seeing the Jhulelal Tirathdham is the closest I will ever get to my beloved Sindh. At long last I had the chance to taste the same salt and walk on the same earth as my ancestors. And I long to return to Jhulelal Tirathdham to experience the wonders of Sindh again.

THE MAIN STATUE AT JHULELAL TIRATHDHAM

16. Teaching Tina

Sindhi mutton, and a course on Sindhi culture

"Tina dear, the marriage ceremony begins at 11am, so you can have a little rest and then get ready."

My niece Tina had arrived early that morning from Canada to spend a fortnight with us before she returned to her parents, and then on to the University of British Columbia to complete her graduation. When IRB and I picked her up from the airport at 3am, she happily announced, "Aunty, Dad said I must learn something about Sindhi culture from you. He says you know everything."

I phoned cousin Kamal as soon as we reached home and gave him a piece of my mind. Never mind what time it was in Canada and whether or not he was busy.

"What instructions have you sent me through your darling daughter? I must teach her something about Sindhi culture? Firstly, you are shirking your own responsibility and secondly, courses in cultural studies are taught over a period of two years! There's nothing I can do in two weeks!"

"You are the Professor, sis, and you know everything. I was born in Calcutta, schooled in Panchgani, flew off to Ohio for my graduation. Moved to Dubai to work for two years. Then to Hong Kong and Singapore. After that, as you know, I came to Canada and met my Bengali wife Mitali, born and raised in Toronto. How would I know anything about Sindhi culture?"

"You should! Your blood is Sindhi, and you were born to Sindhi parents," I scolded him in as firm a tone as I could muster. For Kamal, two years younger than me, has always been like a younger brother. We had spent many happy days together while growing up in Calcutta.

"I'm sure in all the various places I have stayed in, my blood has got diluted. I will soon be heading for Texas as my Sindhi partner says the property market there is booming."

"Before you go off to Texas, take time off to study and then teach Tina something about Sindhi culture."

"Sis, I can't take any time off! Don't you know Sindhis are the original gypsies? And I am one such. It's in my blood."

"Ok, ok," I said, quite amused, "as usual you have all the answers. You haven't changed at all! But what shall I teach her?"

"My dear sis, teach her anything. Don't you remember how you taught me to buy Sindhi mutton? Teach her that."

"I don't remember buying Sindhi mutton! And I don't like going to smelly butcher shops. Anyway, I've become veg. What a strange thing to ask me to do. By the way is that a part of Sindhi culture?"

"Of course it is! It is part of our heritage. I was in New York in the Indian area at Jackson Heights, when a man came to the butchery and asked for 'Sindhi mutton'! I thought the butcher wouldn't understand, but the fellow smiled and replied, 'Yes, of course sir. We have tender mutton chops cut the way Sindhis like'. He was obviously familiar with this special Sindhi cut and quality!"

"Well if that is all you want her to learn, then just take her to Jackson Heights on your next trip!" I suggested as helpfully as I could.

He continued as though he hadn't heard: "I remember that day when Uncle, your dad, was not feeling well and he wanted to eat **photay jo teevan**. He felt it would be good for his sore throat. So we went to the New Market and I told the butcher: 'Aadha killo mutton' and he instantly packed up a parcel in a newspaper and handed it to me. You grabbed it and gave it back to him and announced authoritatively: 'Bak-ree ka nahi, bak-ray ka. Ye jaldi vapas lo. Aur budhe bakray ka nahi. Chhote bakray ka. Aur chops kato!'

You were fourteen, and scrawny. And I was twelve. The butcher laughed shamelessly and stared at you, a chit of a girl, ordering him. You held your ground and refused to budge and pointed to the cut you wanted. Then without uttering a word, he unpacked the parcel and gave us the fresh cuts you had pointed at! When we came home, your dad said the mutton was better than anything he had ever purchased."

"Kamal, you're making this up. I don't remember this incident."

"Cook some **photay jo teevan** and send me some. Then you'll remember. Also **saee bhaji**. A dabba full of each item, please!"

And he rang off.

Torn fishing net

Kamal had done well. His chain of 'Indian Designer Apparel for Real Men' bearing the label 'Maharaja' in four American cities had become a brand. He had picked up the ropes of the business when he had worked in Hong Kong and Singapore. He was now planning to open an outlet in Texas, where there was a large Indian community.

Around 8am, I noticed that Tina had dozed off. So I called

out to her, "The whirring of the aeroplane engine must be still buzzing in your ears, Tina dear. But we'll have to leave by ten. Have you taken out something to wear?"

"Aunt, I brought my expensive Chantilly lace saree specially for Bombay parties," said Tina rubbing her eyes, "I've heard Sindhi weddings are all about dressing up and dripping diamonds and designer handbags and ..."

"My dear, this morning the ceremony is in the Gurdwara and you may have to sit on the floor. So put away your Chantilly for the cocktail party tomorrow at the Taj! Today you can wear something lighter."

"In the Gurdwara?" she asked. "But Aunt, we are not Sikhs or Punjabis. In the USA it is Sikh Punjabis who go to the Gurdwara!"

"I suppose this is what cousin Kamal wants me to teach you," I launched into my mentoring mission immediately. "A Sindhi's religious ideas are a blending of many faiths – Hinduism, Sikhism, Sufism. Guru Nanak came to Sindh several times. Later the other Sikh Gurus also came from Amritsar. There were Gurdwaras in several towns in Sindh. In fact, your dad will tell you that our grandmother, Vanatbai, used to read two pages of the Granth Sahib every morning, and a page from the Sukhmani every evening. All in Gurmukhi."

"Didn't she know English?"

"Tina, our grandmother Vanatbai was born around 1890 in Dali, a small village in Sindh. I don't think anyone there knew any English! She probably didn't go to school. But she must have learnt cooking and stitching and embroidery at home. Most of the families there attended the Gurdwara regularly and listened to the reading of the Granth Sahib and by listening and looking at the script in the holy book, they learnt to read and understand!"

"How clever," said Tina, her eyes shining, "I wish I could learn that way. Aunt, do you know Gurmukhi?"

"No, but I wish I did. Grandmother Vanatbai tried to teach her two sons – my father and Kamal's father. They did learn a little, and then forgot."

"If they didn't learn Gurmukhi, which language did they learn, Aunt?"

"They went to school and they learnt Sindhi. The British had also opened English schools by then. Did you learn about the British Rule in India and Napier's annexation of Sindh in your history course?"

"I'm a History major," replied Tina confidently. "I have learnt about the country being divided into India and Pakistan. And then the mass exodus of the Sindhi Hindus. Aunt, did you also lose your home?"

"Of course. My father and Kamal's father and the whole family left everything and fled to India. We are refugees. But it's a long story. I'll tell you later. We should start getting ready. What are you wearing?'

"Here Aunt, since I am keeping the Chantilly lace for tomorrow, I can wear this other outfit."

Tina took out an elasticated tight black sleeveless tube top, very low at the neck and a fishnet skirt put together with safety pins.

"That skirt? Is it made from a torn fishing net?" I asked, a trifle scandalized.

"Aunt, don't you know the style? I thought Bombay people knew all the styles! It's not made from a torn fishing net. It cost a fortune! Actress Elizabeth Hurley – you must have heard of her. She wore a whole dress made of this fabric, fixed with pins. And..."

"Put that away, Tina! Even when we came as refugees to

India we still had our pride. We wore clean clothes. We washed one set and wore the other set. We darned and stitched our clothes ourselves. We didn't go around in clothes with holes and pins!"

"But Aunt..."

"Don't interrupt. The first thing my mother organized for my sister Mira and me during the school summer holidays were tailoring classes. We were twelve or thirteen, then, and we learnt to stitch our own clothes. My father would always purchase a thaan."

"What's that Aunt?"

"A large roll of cloth. I remember one roll in particular. It was a creamy-beige colour. Father had managed to get a roll of that colour because that was the colour of our school uniform. From that roll, we stitched our school uniforms, shirts were stitched for the boys, my mother got a blouse and saree petticoat, and my grandmother Vanatbai was very happy to get a new *suthan* and *pehran* too. Besides our school uniforms, my sister and I used our creative and patchwork skills, and made ourselves nice dresses to wear to the park in the evenings from that roll!"

"You mean the whole family walked around looking like Tweedledum and Tweedledee wearing the same colour and ..." Tina would not stop laughing.

"Yes my dear, today it all sounds very funny when ready-mades are so affordable and most Sindhi families have done so well that they can buy and wear just about anything they want! But most of us left our homes in Sindh with nothing except the clothes we were wearing. We had no money to buy fancy materials. It was economical to buy the entire bale of 30 or 40 yards in the wholesale market!"

"What else did your parents do, Aunt?" asked Tina who was still trying to control her laughter.

"Well we didn't throw away buttons and hooks. We removed them from the old clothes and stitched them on to new clothes. We used the old clothes to dust and clean. We didn't spend money buying new dusters. I remember removing the zip from one of my father's old trousers and fixing it on to another new pair of trousers which my mother was stitching for him. We Sindhis were always conscious of low carbon footprint – something you youngsters have started understanding only now! But let's hurry up..."

As usual, IRB poked his head in at the wrong moment.

"Listen ladies, you better hurry. You know I don't like being late! And my dear wife, stop criticizing Tina's wardrobe! Let these young people wear what they want and do what they like. If Vandana had listened to your sense of style, she would never have become Miss Beauty Queen at Jai Hind College and then again at Thadomal Shahani Engineering College, the best colleges of Bombay where there are so many of our beautiful and talented Sindhi girls."

Then looking at Tina, he gave her his parting advice: "Beta, you will look nice in whatever you wear."

"Well, I'm not coming to the Gurdwara with my niece dressed in a fishing net fixed with pins! The two of you can go! I'll stay at home."

"Come on sweetheart!" said IRB placatingly. "Try and remember that we are not refugees anymore! You must have collected a suitcase full of buttons and hooks by now. What are you going to do with all that?"

"You never know what you are going to need and when you may need it," I replied defensively.

"Well, the last time I lost a button on my trouser, you opened two suitcases full of buttons and spent half the day searching, but couldn't find one that matched!"

"That is because you are too finicky, Mr B." I always addressed IRB as Mr B when our opinions differed.

"Our Sindhi girls have to keep up with the times. They can't sit collecting buttons and hooks. Vandana has a Master's degree from Cornell – the finest education in the world, followed by an award for women in industry! Must she collect buttons and hooks too? Times have changed and we must change too. Now hurry up and let's leave on time."

And IRB, a stickler for punctuality, headed for his room to get ready too.

"Uncle loves giving long speeches, but I want you to dress properly for the Gurdwara," I told Tina firmly.

"Ok Aunt, I'll wear whatever you say. Mom insisted that I pack this salwar suit. She wore it to a special event when she was pregnant with me twenty years ago."

"Tina, this is perfect. You have to be modestly dressed and cover your head. Where is the matching chunni with this outfit?"

"I think I forgot to pack it. But Aunt, I'll look like grandmother Vanatbai in that. I won't be able to breathe. It covers my arms, my neck and the neck-frill reaches up to my lips! How will I eat?"

"Yes, this is most suitable. Vanatbai always looked nice. I'll show you her photo. A Gurdwara is not a gym or a night club. It's a holy place. Now get ready."

Tina sulked. I ignored her mood. But she was happy at the Gurdwara and enjoyed the langar after the wedding ceremony and even made a few young friends.

New business opportunity

As we were leaving the Gurdwara, we met my 'park friend' Pushpa Bijlani. We hadn't met for quite some time and she waved out to me like a long-lost friend.

"O hello, Laxmi," she said, "Where have you been? Such a long time since we met. You have put on weight but that is ok at your age."

"No I haven't," I said indignantly, "it must be this thick khadi silk saree!" I glared at her, wondering why some Sindhi women spoke like this. Sometimes I'd hear, "Oh you are looking healthy!" which I have never understood. Is this a compliment or an insult? But never one to miss the opportunity to hit back, I countered, "I suppose you have been very busy as usual with your card parties and your kitty parties! And you must have forgotten what I look like."

For some reason, Pushpa Bijlani always called me Laxmi. I would patiently remind her, every time she did so, that my name was Shakun and not Laxmi. After hundreds of failed attempts, I had given up. I suppose I looked like the goddess of wealth to her, and once she even told me that she always won at her kitty club whenever "she had my darshan"! So I kept quiet and decided to feel happy with my new auspicious name.

"No, no, how could I forget how you look! I never forget anything. But first, let me tell you Laxmi, we have kept Path Sahib in the Khatwari Darbar. The Bhog is on Sunday. It is one year since my mother-in-law passed away. You have to come for Bhog and Prasad."

"Of course I will come," I said. "We are such good friends. I even knew your mother-in-law. She used to tell me that her family and my parents were on the same ship, Sonavati, when we were fleeing Pakistan. The little food available on the journey was given to the children. Many of the parents remained hungry. But of course Pushpa, you and I, were too small to remember all this."

"Yes Laxmi, we must have been just two or three years old. My mother used to remember one of the passengers on board the Sonavati on that trip. She was a young pregnant woman, travelling alone because her husband had been unable to get on the ship and had been told to take the next one. Poor thing, she vomited throughout that journey and couldn't eat a thing all the way from Karachi to Gujarat. She must have been so anxious – she suffered a lot."

"Yes. Many suffered during that trip," I replied.

"Thank God now all that is behind us and we can forget those difficult days," she said, adding, "Tell me, Laxmi, who is this pretty girl you have with you? Why don't you bring her also to the Bhog?"

"She is from Canada," I said, "she has come to spend some time with me."

"You must register her."

"Register?" I asked, surprised, "She is already registered for her degree in Canada. After that she wants to do some acting and singing."

"Laxmi, get her married to a nice boy. You have to register her in my matrimonial agency. My neighbour and I have started this agency for social service to the community. After Partition families have lost touch. Our young boys and girls are spread all over the world and they want Sindhi partners. Where are they to find? So for convenience we have opened five files."

"Files?" I inquired.

"Yes. File No. 1 has the professional doctors and engineer boys from foreign who want fair, beautiful, professional

Sindhi girls from India. This file has a list of eligible girls with their photos and qualifications.

"Then there is File No. 2, where we introduce homely Sindhi girls to Sindhi business boys in 'foreign'. And File No. 3 has all the second-marriage candidates.

"Ok, I can see you are in a hurry now," said Laxmi, intercepting a glance between Tina and me. "I will phone and explain the rest of the categories."

As soon as she left, Tina said to me excitedly, "Aunt I want to register!"

"You? You want to get married now? But what about your degree? This is not what you came to Bombay for! Cousin Kamal didn't tell me to introduce you to a suitable boy." I said, quite surprised.

"Aunt, please, please give me her cell number and I will ask this aunty for details. It all sounds so exciting."

"Ok. As soon as we get home, remind me. I suppose you want to learn how Matrimonial Agencies are run here and you can advise Kamal. He is such a great entrepreneur, always on the lookout for new business ideas. I know a Brahman in Colaba, Mohan Maharaj, who performs rituals and ceremonies and also runs a marriage agency: all on-line and fully computerized. He is very 'savvy', they all say. Interviews between boy and girl are arranged by him online for a handsome fee. He has minted money and bought two adjacent flats near his own at Colaba! Yes, let us advise Kamal, and we can become partners."

Mast Qalandar

When I woke the next morning, I heard music and gently tapped on Tina's door. If she was listening to music, she must be awake.

And she was.

She was dancing to the music of Runa Laila's 'Mast Qalandar' and singing along with it. And I must say she had a melodious voice.

"I love that song Tina. I'm so glad you are listening to devotional music."

Tina stopped and looked at me surprised:

"Devotional, is it? I didn't know that, Aunt."

I sang a few lines to her, even though I am no singer and most of the time I am off-tune:

> O laal meri pat rakhiyo bhala Jhoole Laalan
> Sindhri da, Shewan da sakhi shahbaz Qalandar
> Ali da pehla number ...

"Aunt, your voice is quite good and ..."

"Not really, it was better before, but I want to tell you that there are three holy personages here: First comes Jhulelal. You can see his picture in my pooja room.

Then there is mention of the Sufi Saint Lal Shahbaz Qalandar, a preacher of tolerance and understanding between Hindus and Muslims. And lastly, there is the mention of Ali, son-in-law of the Prophet Muhammad, who is considered the master of the Sufis."

"Aunt, you really know a lot. No wonder Dad insisted I should visit you."

"There is much more to this song. But I have work to do now. Do sing it once again. I love your voice."

As Tina started singing, IRB seeing her door wide open came in and sat down to listen. When she had finished, he stood up and clapped.

"Tina," he said, "there is a Music Evening next week at the Willingdon Club. I'm going to suggest your name to sing

'Mast Qalandar'. The organizers at our club have planned the evening so that members come to understand different communities. You can talk about Sindh."

"Uncle I can sing. But I really don't know what I should say about Sindh!"

"Your Aunt will help you. She is very good at these things! She has been lecturing to me and to the college students since the last God knows how many decades. That's how I know so much. She even got a Best Teacher Award – not from me, but from the government!"

We all laughed and then IRB said: "Shakun, don't you like my idea?"

"Sweetheart," I said, "your ideas are always brilliant! I am sure you will go to the club tomorrow and start singing Tina's praises to all your cronies. Then your buddies will have no option but to attend."

"Of course they will attend. And I'll invite them for a drink in the pub downstairs after the performance. It's all settled."

And then IRB, master of the art of good management and outsourcing, walked out and left us to work out the nitty-grittys of the program.

"Aunt, what do I do? I don't know anything about Sindh."

"Tina, you will learn fast, and it will be a great experience for you. Cousin Kamal will be thrilled."

"How do I learn so quickly? What do I say? I don't want to make a laughingstock of myself."

"You won't! Just relax! I'll write a short essay on Sindh for you. Read it at least once every night for four nights. Then you will remember everything and feel quite confident. That's a study mantra, a 'mnemonic device'. That's the way I taught Vandana to study and speak at elocution competitions. I'll write ..."

"But Aunt ..."

"I'll write out the translation of 'Mast Qalandar' for you this evening and some notes on Sindh, and keep the paper on the dining table. You can start your study tonight."

Tina smiled and gave me a hug: "Tusi 'great' hai, Aunty!" Clearly she knew more Indianisms than one would have expected.

Damadam Mast Qalandar, with translation

My Breath Sings for the Saint

O laal meri pat rakhiyo bhala Jhoole Laalan
Oh Lal Qalandar and Jhulelal, may I always have your divine protection

Sindhri da, Shewan da sakhi shahbaz Qalandar
Friend and sire of Sindh and Sehwan

Ali da pehla number

Lord Ali comes before everything

Char chirag tere baran hamesha
Your shrine is always lit with four lamps

Panjva main baaran aayi bhala Jhoole Laalan
Lord, here I come to light the fifth lamp

...repeat

Sindri da sehvan da, sakhi shabaaz Qalandar

Hindh sindh peera teri naubat vaaje

Your heroic name rings across Hind and Sindh

Naal vaje ghadiyaal bala jhoole laalan

Let the gongs ring loud and clear

for your glory day and night

Points for Tina's talk

'Qalandar' is a title given to a seeker who is seen to have achieved a very high level of spirituality. And 'Mast Qalandar' is also called Shah-Baz or 'falcon', because he assumed that shape in order to set free a saint who had been pierced with a sharp instrument by an infidel king on suspicion of sorcery.

A secular people

We Sindhis lived in the province of Sindh. But because of Partition by our erstwhile British rulers in 1947, Sindh became part of the newly-formed Islamic state of Pakistan. Sindhi Hindus became refugees overnight without any homeland even though they had lived in harmony with Muslims in Sindh. The Hindus were broadminded and tolerant of the people of every religion and faith they encountered. They participated in the worship of the saints and pirs – spiritual guides – of the Muslims. Quite often they became their murids – followers.

Colonial writers observed that the Hindu religion was not to be found in 'a state of purity' in Sindh. The ancient Vedantic wisdom of the Hindu faith allowed for great freedom of thought and expression and coexistence of vastly different customs and traditions and the Hinduism of Sindh had evolved into a fine blend which incorporated Islam, Sufism and Sikhism.

Jhulelal and the spirituality of the Indus

Sindh was a dry and rainless land. But with our great 'Sindhu Nadi' flowing through it, the Sindhis never felt any want. Our water God Uderolal, also called Jhulelal, was represented in human form sitting with their legs crossed, on a flower spread over a fish.

While a large percentage of our people were Nanakpanthis, the principal religion of the Hindus was the Indus cult – adoration of Darya Sahib, the river which sustained the people. Its inundations assured them of a regular food supply and without this holy river, Sindh would have been a desert. They celebrated all their festivals on the banks of the river and prayed here for all their needs. On festival days such as New Year's, and on the new moon, people sang and danced and took out a *behrano* and performed a dance referred to as *chhej*.

Many myths and legends centred around Jhulelal-Uderolal. When the Hindus of Sindh were harassed during the reign of the tyrannical Mirkshah (of whom, incidentally, no historical record exists), Jhulelal was said to have saved them. The Muslims too worshipped the same water god, as Khwaja Khizr. He was also known by other names such as Zinda Pir and Darya Lal.

THE SHRINE OF JHULELAL, LOCATED NEAR TANDO ADAM
IMAGE COURTESY ZULFIQAR ALI KALHORO

Jhulelal occupied the thoughts of the innumerable traders of Sindh who had to cross the Arabian Sea for their trading activities: the Sindhworkis had to sail to several ports and sell their wares, the textiles and handwork that Sindh was known for. The Shikarpuris with their banking system and hundi-business had agents in several cities of Central Asia. The rich Bhaibands had offices in ports around the world.

Shah Abdul Latif sang of the young brides who stood by the sacred river, emotionally wrought and sad, as their husbands left them to sail away short weeks after they were wed. They knew the men would return only at the end of their **müsafri** – the period of three to five years away working in a distant land. Heavy-hearted, they stood by the river praying and making **akho** – offerings – for their safe return.

There are several Sindhi **pahakas** associated with the river. When one wants to bless someone, one says: **Jhülelal bera paar** – may you have a safe journey on the seas with the blessing of Jhulelal. On the other hand, **Beri büdaee** – may your boat sink – may be uttered in anger or frustration.

Sufism

The highly blended faith which flourished in Sindh and which was followed by Hindus and Muslims alike was Sufism.

Sufi is derived from the word 'safu' which means 'clean' or 'pure'. Some hold that it may have come from the Arabic word 'suf' meaning 'wool'. Pious men practicing austerity wandered across to Sindh from Persia, Turkey and neighbouring countries, robed in rough woollen shawls. They began to be called 'sufis'

One of the most famous Sufi Pirs was Lal Shahbaz

Qalandar who was born Usman Marwandi (1177-1274). He was a wandering poet-singer, a grammarian, celibate, and revered as a saint, who preached religious tolerance among Muslims and Hindus. He died in Sehwan, and is enshrined there.

The essence of the doctrine of Sufism is: "You yourself are the one you seek". The seer and the seeker are one. There is a Sufi allegory which explains this concept (cited by Popati Hiranandani):

> Once birds of all kinds decided to find their king Simurgha, the bird with the golden wings. They flew towards the valley where Simurgha lived. They left behind all those who were tired or tempted with luxuries on the way. Thirty of them reached the valley. When they descended, they found that their wings had turned golden and they were themselves the Simurgha – the flock of thirty.

This One-ness of the Creator and the Created is described in allegorical terms by Shah Abdul Latif, the most well-known of the Sufi poets. He expresses this concept beautifully when he writes:

> He is nearer to me than the pupil of my eyes.

And then again:

> Goliyan – goliyan – na – lahan.
> *Let me not find Him even if I seek Him.*

Almost every Sufi order traces its lineage to Hazrat Ali, son-in-law of Prophet Muhammad, who features in our beloved folk ballad Damadam Mast Qalandar.

Wine and intoxicants

When one loves intensely and forgets oneself, one finds Him and His beauty. Among Hindus the use of bhang – marijuana – is prevalent among the devotees of Lord Shiva.

The Sufis too, permit the use of wine as it has the property of loosening the unconscious forces and producing a state of religious ecstasy. The ceremonies of Sufism consist of music and dancing. Sufis staunchly believe that the path to the Beautiful and the Divine traverses trance and ecstasy.

The tomb cult

The logic behind the innumerable tombs in Sindh is interesting. The Muslims buried their dead and they believed that the saint or Pir after he was free from the bondage of the body acquired the power to perform miracles and help his followers.

Archaeologist Henry Cousens wrote in his book *Antiquities of Sindh* (1925):

> Sindh is a land of sepulchres and dust ... it has been a country very fruitful in the production of pirs or holy men ... and contains according to the current estimate, no less than 100,000 tombs of saints and martyrs.

Hindus also prayed at the tombs of their Pirs.

The necropolis of Mian Nasir Muhammad Kalhoro in Khairpur
Image courtesy Zulfiqar Ali Kalhoro

Sikhism

The followers of Guru Nanik who came to Sindh brought with them the tenets of Sikhism, and the Sindhis accepted their beliefs and became known as Nanak Panthis: those who followed the peaceful path of Guru Nanak. That is why the Sindhi *tikanas* – temples – always have a photo of Guru Nanak alongside the pictures and idols of the Hindu pantheon of gods. A *bawa* – caretaker – of the temple reads ceremoniously from the Granth Sahib, the holy book of the Sikhs, every morning and then again in the evening.

At Lakhpat, a town on the border of India and Pakistan, one can see a large battalion of the Indian Border Security Force. The highlight of Lakhpat is its beautiful Gurdwara. Guru Nanak is said to have begun his travels in Lakhpat, and visited it several times. The Gurdwara was built at the site where he generally resided, and this Gurdwara preserves in its exhibition cupboard his *chakhris* – wooden footwear. Lakhpat provides a sense of the vista and fragrance of Sindh.

Many Sindhi families follow Sikh rituals and prayers; many have the custom of adding 'Singh' after the name of their firstborn son. Orthodox customs such as growing the hair and wearing a *kara* are not strictly observed by Sindhi Nanakpanthis. It should be noted that it was the British census that categorized Sikhs and Hindus as different, and introduced the suggestion of division between the two communities.

Letter from aunt: conclusion

Tina my dear,

I have written a brief explanation of the lines of the song for you so that you can explain what it means. When you deliver your talk, you don't need to explain every word and line. But once you yourself have understood the gist, you will be able to communicate its essence confidently. As you know, a lawyer who has not done his homework takes ninety minutes to present the facts of the case. But a lawyer who has studied the matter thoroughly can deliver the same matter in nine minutes. By the time you finish reading what I have written, you will also be able to teach your father about Sindh and Sindhi culture.

Best of luck, and prepare well! You have just one week before the program at the Willingdon Sports Club which Uncle is organizing for you.

Aunt

(as always, the Professor)

Popular poster of Lal Shahbaz Qalandar in contemplation and in the movement of dance

17. Brick by brick

THEY RESTORED THEIR FORTUNES

The man was struggling to buy a plot soon after his arrival in Bombay. He didn't have much money, and he knew it would be difficult. But he walked around day after day, in the blazing sun and in the pouring rain, meeting people to get permissions and certificates, looking for a place which was affordable and where his dream could be materialized.

He had been a college professor in Sindh, known for his commitment to education as well as his prowess at sports. A refugee in Bombay, he had stayed in touch with his old colleagues writing postcards to them regularly and telling them that they would soon have to be back to do the work they did at their old college in Sindh. Most thought the man was dreaming. Where was the money? They had become refugees overnight. Some had taken up other jobs to make a living. Some had taken up tutoring young kids in affluent families. The good old days were gone forever. Partition had lost them their homeland, Sindh.

My uncle and aunt were also on a search. Arriving in Bombay after Partition, the family had managed to get accommodation at Nutan Nagar opposite the Bandra station. But there were too many people cramped in that little flat. Looking around, they came across an affordable plot not far from Nutan Nagar.

Bandra, in those days, was a distant, unfashionable suburb with vast open swampy and muddy spaces, and the occasional pig sauntering along its kachha roads. But it was the best they could afford on their budget. They took it up. And one day they noticed the man. He was negotiating the larger plot on the opposite side of the road.

Soon my uncle and aunt began to construct a small bungalow on their plot. My aunt would arrive every afternoon with her little packet of lunch and sit there and supervise the workers. She knew that if she was not physically present, the work would go slow and the workers would waste time and the house would never get built. My uncle, the late Justice J L Nain, was busy struggling with his infant legal practice.

The work in the opposite plot too had begun. The man arrived every day to oversee his construction. They soon began to help each other. Sometimes my aunt would share her lunch with him. When the gentleman's construction was held up because his supply of cement and bricks had been delayed, he would borrow materials from my aunt's stock. And the same procedure was followed when my aunt's construction materials were delayed, as they often were, in the era of shortages that our brand-new nation was facing.

They became friends. He confided to my aunt that some Sindhworkis were helping him with funds. He himself didn't have much. His wife too had sold some of her jewellery to fund the construction. Sometimes my aunt would see him lifting bricks and cement himself, when workers didn't turn up or were too slow. He was impatient to finish the work as soon as possible.

This man was Khushiram Motiram Kundnani. He had left Hyderabad – and had carried his beloved college, Dayaram Jethmal National College, with him – the same college where IRB's uncle Hiralal Bharvani had been Principal. All he needed was a piece of land and a building, and he was making those arrangements now. One of his generous supporters was Barrister Hotchand Advani, a senior lawyer in Sindh, who now passed the hat around to his many affluent Bhaiband clients. They contributed generously to the building of the college.

A TRULY NATIONAL INSTITUTION: PRINCIPAL KUNDNANI ADDRESSES A GATHERING OF THE KANNADA ASSOCIATION AT NATIONAL COLLEGE, BOMBAY, C1955

FROM *THE AMILS OF SINDH* (2019) BY SAAZ AGGARWAL

Kundnani retained the name, with just a minor change to distinguish it from the college left behind: it would be Rishi Dayaram National College.

The first student to apply for admission was a Muslim. When faced with resistance from colleagues, Principal Kundnani replied, "This is National College. Let us never forget that. We will provide education without ever discriminating on the basis of religion, caste or community." The young student, Shakir Gaya, had just Rs20 in his pocket, not enough for the fees. Kundnani admitted him with permission to pay the balance later. This gracious act from someone who had so

> recently faced the brunt of religious discrimination and Partition moved Shakir Gaya deeply. In later years he served National College as professor and always counted Kundnani as a friend and mentor.
>
> *Excerpted from* The Amils of Sindh *(2019) by Saaz Aggarwal*

RD National College was the first of the HSNCB (Hyderabad Sindh National Collegiate Board). HSNCB now has twenty-five educational institutions, and these include not just Science, Commerce and Arts colleges but also colleges of Law, Management Studies, Teachers' Training, Pharmacy, Electronics Engineering, and Computer Technology. Some of the gracious benefactors whose donations realised the founding of these institutes were Wassiamal Assomull, Kishinchand Chellaram, Hassaram Rijhumal, Mithibai Motiram Kundnani, Chandibai Himathaml Mansukhani, KM Kundnani, Gopaldas Jhamatmal Advani, Watumull, Thadomal Shahani, Smt SH Mansukhani, Dr Lakhumal Hiranand, Nari Gursahani, Hashmatrai and Gangaram Himathmal Mansukhani, and many more who remain unnamed.

The Thadomal Shahani Engineering College

The college which holds a special place in my heart is the Thadomal Shahani Engineering College (TSEC) in Bandra. I think all Sindhis should go down on bended knees and bow in gratitude to this institution as it has done yeoman service in helping our bright youngsters to become engineers and 'techies'. As soon as the Government of Maharashtra gave permission for private engineering colleges to be set up, the HSNCB seized the opportunity. Kishinchand Thadomal Shahani, one of the simplest and most unassuming of men whose philosophy of life always seemed to be "You have not lived today until you have done something for someone," came forward. The Thadomal Shahani Trust, named after his father, provided the necessary funds.

TSEC is like a mini-Sindh, and many Sindhi boys and girls have found their life-partners here. So there is love and learning in this institute and there is no need to register at matrimonial agencies! Most children of my family and extended family have graduated from this college, including my daughter and son-in-law. All have done well in the corporate world. And some have initiated successful start-ups which have made valuable contributions to the world of cutting-edge technology. Dada Kishinchand's Shahani Resort in Lonavala, the haven he founded for Sindhis to rest and recover at a moderate cost, is his other gift to the community. The *saee bhaji* and *beeha* – lotus root – *pakoras* served here will bring back nostalgic memories of the dishes made by your grandmother!

Role-model refugees

The scene of the departing Sindhi refugees from Pakistan is described vividly by Sri Prakasa, then India's first High Commissioner to Pakistan:

> "... parties of Hindus started arriving in Karachi from various spots in the interior of the province. They had to stay in Karachi for a few days before they could be transported ... I must pay my tribute to my Sindhi brothers and sisters for keeping up their cheerful spirits even when they were on their way to unknown destinations ... Train journeys were full of danger as they were being attacked, air journeys were expensive. Voyage by sea was the only way by which these migrating people could go ..."

Politicians did not give much support to the Sindhis.

Jawaharlal Nehru once wrote to the 'Nightingale of India', Sarojini Naidu: "I don't know Sindh. I don't feel attracted to it." So a province which was far away, was considered an unattractive and unimportant place for unattractive and unimportant people, and could be simply left behind for Pakistan.

There was a high mortality rate after Partition too. Refugees suffered from trauma and depression after being herded out, often in the middle of the night. One such casualty was my own maternal grandfather, Hardasmal Makhijani, who died soon after arriving in Delhi. A well-to-do landowner and zamindar in his village of Bhiria, he could not bear the cramped and unsanitary conditions of the refugee camp, and the sheer despair of not knowing how he would support his family. My elder cousin and my brothers still remember him as a dignified gentleman, seating them on his favourite camel, and taking them around his fields as his peasants and workers bowed to him in greeting.

My nani Tehemal bai Makhijani (died 1971) and nana hardasmal Makhijani (died 1951)
Courtesy their grandson Jai Prakash Makhijani

The shortage of housing was the first major problem our refugee community faced in Bombay. With some support from the government, they began building homes for themselves in which their own families and those close to them were accommodated at cost. These cooperative housing societies provided housing not just for our community but for others too in need of accommodation. The early buildings such as the Navjivan Cooperative Housing Societies, Nanik Nivas and many others were built by Sindhi 'refugees' evicted from Sindh. Today some Sindhis still live in them but many are occupied by people of other communities.

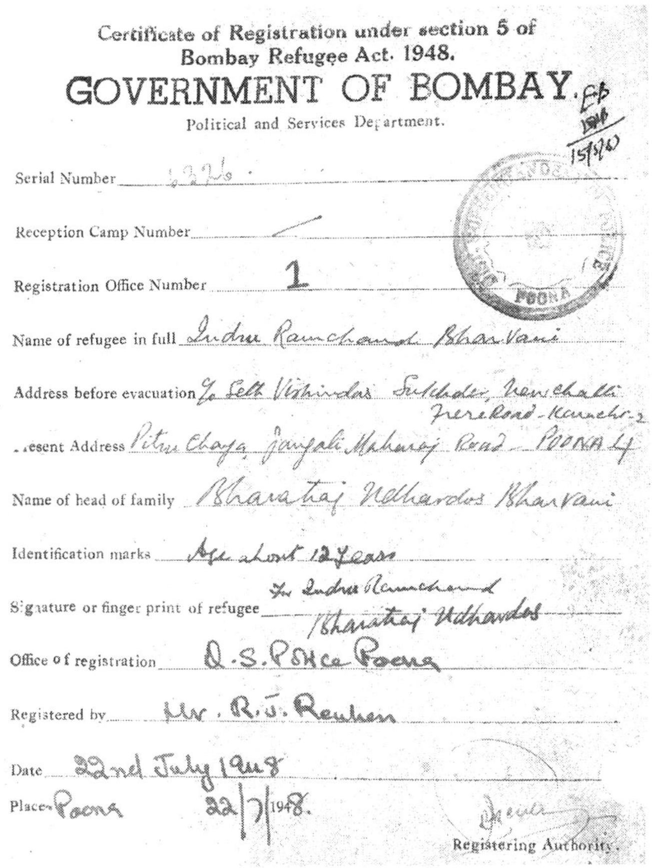
Certificate of Registration under section 5 of
Bombay Refugee Act. 1948.

GOVERNMENT OF BOMBAY.

Political and Services Department.

Serial Number [illegible]

Reception Camp Number —

Registration Office Number 1

Name of refugee in full Indru Ramchand Bharvani

Address before evacuation C/o Seth Vishindas Sukhdev, New Challi, Frere Road - Karachi - 2

Present Address Pitru Chaya, Jangali Maharaj Road, POONA 4

Name of head of family Bharatraj Udharodas Bharvani

Identification marks Age about 12 years

Signature or finger print of refugee for Indru Ramchand / Bharatraj Udharodas

Office of registration Q.S. Police Poona

Registered by Mr. R.J. Reuben

Date 22nd July 1948

Place Poona 22/7/1948.

Registering Authority.

THE CERTIFICATE REGISTERING MY HUSBAND INDRU (REFERRED TO AS 'IRB' IN THIS BOOK) AS A REFUGEE. INDRU WAS BORN IN KARACHI IN 1938. WITHOUT THIS REGISTRATION, THE GOVERNMENT OF BOMBAY STATE HAD THE POWER, UNDER SECTION 5 OF THE BOMBAY REFUGEE ACT, 1948, TO REMOVE PEOPLE SEEKING NEW HOMES BECAUSE THEY HAD BEEN DISPLACED BY PARTITION, FROM ANY CAMP, PLACE OR AREA IN THE STATE. THE CERTIFICATE WAS NECESSARY FOR SCHOOL ADMISSION.

After setting up educational institutions and cooperative housing societies, our role-model refugees went on to creating institutions of public health. In the 1960s, the establishment of large private hospitals was not common, but the idea of the Jaslok Hospital was conceptualized and made a reality by its founders Seth Lokoomal Chanrai and his wife Jasotibai. Seth Lokoomal's vision was implemented and brought to reality largely by his brother-in-law Dada Mathradas Assomull. A stalwart of the Bhaiband community, a gentleman to his fingertips, he always walked ramrod straight, clad in a neat white safari suit, and carried a beautifully sculpted walking stick. I remember him vividly: slim and wiry, a person of medium height but one who stood tall and conscientious when asked to take up any philanthropic assignment. Jaslok Hospital was inaugurated on 6 July 1973 by the then Prime Minister Indira Gandhi. It has beds reserved for the weaker sections of society.

The INLAKS Hospitals in Mumbai and Pune, the Chellaram super-specialty hospital for the treatment of Diabetes in Pune; Raheja Hospital and Hinduja Hospitals in Mumbai, are among Mumbai's multispecialty hospitals. They offer the finest in medical care and advanced medical facilities with highly qualified, skilled doctors.

National anthem

Given the solid contribution from the Sindhi community to the welfare of the country, it is ironical that petitions have been filed twice to remove the word 'Sindh' from the national anthem of India on the grounds that Sindh is no longer a part of India. This was felt as a gross insult by Sindhis everywhere. In an interview to *The Times of India*, well-known criminal lawyer Ram Jethmalani quipped : "The irony is that if such an issue is to be raised at all, it should be raised by Pakistan, not us," adding, "Sindhis may be stateless but they are still live representatives of this civilization. Sindhis glow with pride when they hear the word 'Sindh'. Do you want to take that away too?"

'Minority' status

Sindhis as a community have never asked for reservations. When, as refugees, they needed good-quality education for their children – they did not beseech the government to make arrangements for them. They simply built their own colleges and created huge education infrastructure which was availed of by the entire population and not just the Sindhi community. But when the community wanted reserved seats for Sindhi children – it was refused! It took a long and relentless battle by Dada Nari Gursahani, a renowned lawyer and philanthropist, to win 'minority' status for the colleges built by Partition refugees. Today thousands of Sindhi families have received specific 'community' benefits from these colleges. But this happened only after tens of thousands belonging to other communities had already benefitted.

Integrating, not merely getting absorbed

Our Sindhi colleges have a large mainstream student body as well as a good percentage of young Sindhi students. We can utilize this opportunity to initiate the younger generation into the culture and history of their community, so that they can take pride in the inspiring stories and unwavering optimism of their ancestors.

As educators, it is an opportunity for us to groom them and inculcate in them the desire to learn the language and speak it fluently. Just as we allot 10 extra marks for Sports or NCC, we can allot 10 extra marks for those who offer a paper or project on the history or literature or culture or even cuisine of Sindh. Lectures on the Partition period and its impact on our community, the diaspora during the pre-Partition and post-Partition periods and the identity of Sindhis can be arranged in our colleges periodically. An essay-writing competition centred around some aspect of the geographical position of Sindh and how this determined the mind-set and religious eclecticism of our community can be instituted in colleges and prizes awarded. The philanthropists of our community will willingly contribute generously towards these prizes.

Young Sindhis will learn about our heritage of poetry and literature, of Shah Abdul Latif, Sachal Sarmast, Sami and others; our folk tales, our legends, and our proverbs which express age-old wisdom and common sense so picturesquely. One of IRB's favourites, which I can't resist quoting here, was **baa ta baarah**: when two people bond, they have the strength of twelve. Another family favourite, **peta mae soor aathas** literally means 'pain in the belly'; metaphorically it describes someone itching for a bribe. Youngsters must be introduced to the colour and wit of their mother tongue!

Phoenix, flamingo and chameleon

After Partition, Sindhis quickly adapted to local conditions. In South India, Sindhis speak Tamil, Malayalam, Kannada or Telugu. In Spain, they speak Spanish; in China they speak Chinese. Harkrishin becomes Harry, Jaikishin becomes Jackson, Sunder becomes Sunny, Shyam becomes Sam and Indru becomes Andrew. Just as the phoenix rose from its own ashes, so did we. And like chameleons, we reinvented ourselves to blend in wherever we settled!

One interesting phenomena of my community is the return

of the prodigal! Towards the end of the year, like a flock of colourful flamingoes descending on Bombay in winter, the Sindhis arrive from every corner of the globe. Bag and baggage, diamonds and designer sarees, Gucci and Gabbana, they come eager to socialize and flaunt their finery at weddings, funerals, card parties at the club, and to indulge in Bombay street food. They visit relatives, catch up on all the gossip, register their sons and daughters at matrimonial agencies, and make pious pilgrimages to their 'gurus' and places of religious importance. Most special are the trips to well-known humanitarian and charitable organizations where their names will be printed in bold letters as big donors.

Sindhis are called ostentatious, showy and vulgar and described in much the same manner as Shakespeare's Portia contemptuously described one of her undesirable suitors in *The Merchant of Venice*:

> I think he bought his doublet (jacket) in Italy, his
> round hose (breeches) in France, his bonnet (hat)
> in Germany and his behaviour everywhere.

For Sindhis to flaunt their worldly possessions and attire purchased in cities across the globe is surely a privilege they are entitled to? After all, they have made it from nothing. For many it is very much a rags to riches story. From refugee-dom to real-estate tycoons, from residing in camps to residing in super-deluxe 7-star luxury hotels! It's been hard work all the way up but success has followed. They gained a lot – but what they lost they will never look back to or mourn for.

18. The bomb that got me started

Bizarre though this may sound, it was the World Trade Centre bombing in 2001 that inspired me to explore my Sindhi roots.

This bombing was an event that changed the world, creating two distinct eras: pre- and post-WTC bombing. It changed our perspective of the world, and made us suddenly cognizant of the subhuman, barbaric streak that exists in human nature.

It so happened that in 2001 I had been selected for a Fulbright teaching program to the USA. I was very excited that I had been selected by the prestigious Fulbright Foundation, and was looking forward to a totally new experience. I had previously done brief teaching stints in London where I had found students receptive to courses on 'Indians Writing in English'. Quite a few had ancestors who had served in India, and learning about India was an exhilarating experience for them. The classes were always very lively and interactive. I knew that with American students, things would be different. And so they were.

I was to start at the City University of New York (CUNY) on Tuesday, 11 September 2001. I had arrived in New York a few days in advance, on a Saturday, and my daughter Vandana had come to pick me up at the airport. She had recently been awarded her Master's degree from Cornell and had taken up a job which entailed frequent travel. Since this necessitated staying in hotels, she had accumulated multiple free points for hotel stays. What better opportunity to use some of these points than when Mother was visiting!

Both of us enjoyed the luxury hotel stay at Hotel Millennium for two nights, while we looked around for an apartment where I could stay during the three months of my teaching program at CUNY. An apartment close to the financial district of New York and within walking distance of the WTC seemed to be the ideal choice and we did locate one at John Street. Leaving my luggage there, we went to spend the weekend with IRB's Uncle Rattan at Great Neck, a toney suburb of New York. I was to pick up the keys to the apartment on Tuesday morning. As Vandana left to return to her project in Georgia on Monday, she said: "Mom, you must go right up the WTC and see the view from there. It's breathtaking. Quite an experience, and the highlight of the city."

On the morning of Tuesday, 11 September, I rose early and said my daily prayer. I was going to face a new environment, live in an apartment in the heart of the financial district of New York, and be totally on my own. Bright and early I left with Uncle Rattan who was taking the train to Penn Station from where his office was a five-minute walk.

As our train approached Penn Station, we heard announcements which indicated a freak accident near the WTC. A few minutes later it was reported that this was not an accident but a terrorist attack. It was not clear what exactly had happened.

As we stepped out of the station, Uncle Rattan suggested I accompany him to his office till we knew whether it was safe for me to go to John Street to pick up my keys from the Brazilian student whose apartment I was renting while he was away on a study tour in Europe.

When we walked into Uncle Rattan's office complex, we

saw that every TV was switched on. People were glued to their phones, looking anxious and disoriented, trying to contact their loved ones. Vandana phoned from Georgia to tell me that they had got an alert and their meeting had been put on hold. Nobody knew what was going to happen next.

There was no news from CUNY. No news from the Brazilian in John Street about the keys he was to hand to me, or about my luggage which was lying in his apartment. I wondered if he had managed to leave before the bomb blast occurred. Uncle Rattan generously assured me that I must stay on at Great Neck for as long as I needed to. I could wear his wife Bina's clothes (she was twice my size)!

I will never forget the trauma of seeing the cordoned off area of the WTC at close quarters, a few days later. Security staff wearing masks were moving around, cleaning up, sorting debris. A smell of burning flesh permeated the air. I had managed to contact the Brazilian and he had been close to tears as he related to me how he had rushed out of his house that day in his underwear. The first thing he remembered was the rattling of his windows, and how the building had begun to sway, as in a high-intensity earthquake. Along with the other residents of the building he had managed to rush out. He was presently staying with a friend. So there was going to be some delay in retrieving my luggage and returning my advance payment. His trip was off, and he was not sure how long he would have to camp with friends. Like me, he was clearly also using borrowed clothes.

I had heard nothing from CUNY and decided to visit. The first thing I saw when I entered was a large poster on the bulletin board in the lobby. The poster showed a neatly-drawn map on which were clearly marked the following places: Afghanistan, Kandahar, Kabul and Quetta. Below the map in bold letters was printed:

> Anyone with knowledge of Pashto, please phone
> ... or report to Room No 1 on the ground floor.

I stared at the poster, my eyes feasting on the map and on the names of these familiar places which I had heard from my parents' lips so often. I had never bothered to look them up on a map before. Two years after my father's demise, I was standing in the university foyer, staring at a map labelled with names of places familiar to him, and I felt I could clearly hear his voice speaking in Pashto. Standing there, fond memories of my father washed over me.

Why did he visit these places where he spoke Pashto? And what compelled him to leave them behind? Oh how

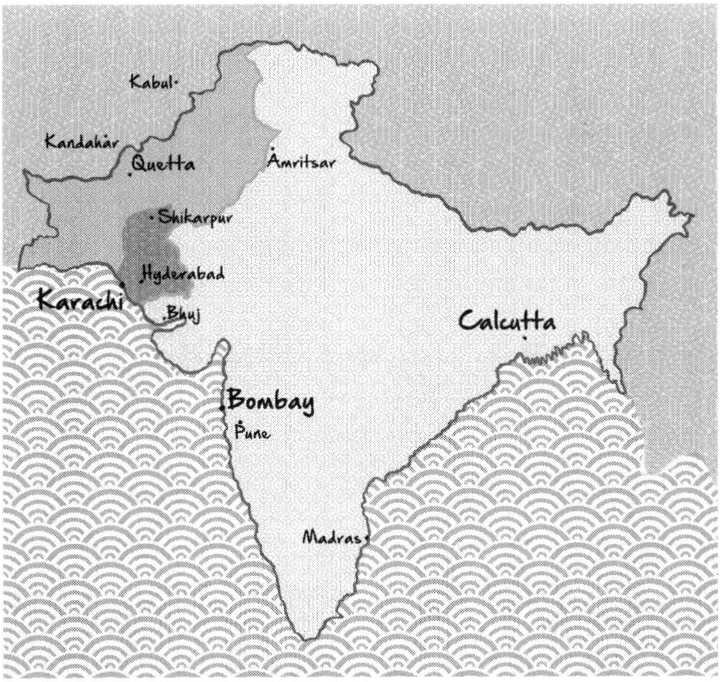

SPATIAL REPRESENTATION OF INDIA AND ITS SURROUNDING AREAS IN 1947, INDICATING SOME OF THE PLACES MENTIONED IN THIS BOOK

sad he was to never again revisit and meet old friends, and speak the language he felt so comfortable with! He conversed using those strange and interesting-sounding words with the dry-fruit merchants in the New Market at Calcutta. I wish I had learnt something of them from him!

How had my father learnt Pashto? When I returned home to India, I went to visit my brothers Ashok and Ajit in Calcutta, who were a few years older than me, and asked them to tell me whatever they could remember. This was the first step of my journey into Sindh.

Before the Partition of India in 1947, my father ran a flourishing tea-trading business in Quetta. He was born in Dali, a village in the Nawabshah district of Sindh. When he was twenty-four, his marriage was arranged with Parvati, a girl of fifteen from Bhiria, an adjacent village not too far off. It was a quick arranged marriage as his elder brother and her elder sister were already married. So it was all in the family and both sides felt secure in the knowledge that the families were already known to each other.

Big cities attract the young. And that is why my parents left Dali and came to Quetta where my father started tea-trading. He imported tea from Calcutta and sold it in Kabul. He brought back pomegranates, dry fruits and other popular items from Kabul, and traded them in Quetta. It was during his travels in these cities that he had learnt Pashto.

As a child growing up in Calcutta, it never occurred to me to enquire why we had left these places. I did not understand the word 'Partition' even though I heard the family refer to it so often: "Before Partition, when we stayed in Quetta, it was so cold. We used to have fireplaces and sit and eat walnuts and dry fruits. Here in Calcutta the quality of fruit is so ordinary and ..."

Then my father would reminisce about his dear old friend,

Lekhraj, who lived in Kandahar and whom he would meet on his frequent visits there.

"Was Kandahar close by?" I at age five would ask innocently.

"Not too far," replied my father." Sometimes I even managed to go in a horse carriage through the Bolan Pass and trade my cartons of soap, tea, and a few other articles, and return with bags of dry fruits. Kandahar had very good fruits."

The Kandahari fruit-traders were a recognizable group in the dry fruit section of Calcutta's New Market, with their ruddy complexions, well-built figures, and their baggy shalwar-kurtas. Their stalls were at the extreme end of the market and they would respond with joy and enthusiasm when a local spoke to them in their own language. And as we walked away, father would tell us, with a faraway look in his eyes, "Parts of Afghanistan are desert areas. It's a different life out there."

In school I hated Geography. Afghanistan and Balochistan meant nothing to me. I found it difficult to even remember whether Calcutta was in the East or in the West of India. Bombay of course, fascinated me because a number of my father's relations lived there. But the names Kandahar, Quetta and Chaman were often on my parents' lips. Chaman was the place from where the currants and kissmiss (raisins) came. The distance between Quetta and Chaman was not much. "The grapes we used to get from Chaman were so much more tasty than those we get here in Calcutta."

And whenever some news arrived from Mr Lekhraj in Kandahar, my father's eyes would light up and he would say, "After you children finish learning English and Bengali, you must learn Pashto!" How I wish I had.

19. Some precious memories from members of my family

How I became a brown sahib

As narrated by my brother, Dr Ashok Nain

I was born in Karachi, Sindh, and spent the major part of my very early years in Quetta, a beautiful place which today is better known for bombs than the fruit we knew and loved it for.

Here, my father was a tea merchant who purchased tea from eastern India, brought it to Quetta to blend and reprocess, and then exported it to Iran, Iraq and Afghanistan, and also sold it locally in the extreme north western areas of Undivided India. My very early years were happy years, and I learnt to speak the local languages of Pashto, Urdu and Sindhi. My father would disappear for several days at a time, and I would wonder where he was. When he came back he would tell us children about his visits to Ispahan, Tehran, Kabul, Dera Ghazi Khan, the Khyber Pass and other exotic-sounding places. Oh how I wished that one day I too would visit these magical places!

Had things continued as they were, perhaps today I would have been a very different person, from a completely different culture, and with a completely different vision of life and the world. However, the dream was shattered. India was partitioned.

Quetta in those days had only a handful of Hindu families. We had to leave or convert, or perhaps face the sword. My father did the most convenient thing by sending the family to my uncle in Karachi and stayed on until he could sell off all the assets and collect money from those who owed him, after which he joined us in Karachi. But Karachi too was not safe for us and very soon all of us cousins, brothers, aunts, uncles and grandparents had to leave by steamer from Karachi to Jam Khambalia in Gujarat. Here we stayed for some time in a dharamshala and ultimately my father, who had stayed back in Karachi, arrived and took us, my mother and siblings and me, to live in Calcutta. He had chosen to settle in Calcutta because he had been in the tea business, and it was a good business to be in, and Calcutta was the Mecca of tea. However, things in Calcutta were not easy. Several lakhs of people from East Pakistan were flooding the city as refugees. My father had business contacts in eastern India, and came up with a novel idea. We all became citizens of Tripura. In those days, Tripura was an independent princely state with its own Maharaja. However, our Tripura citizenship did not last very long. The state of Tripura merged with the Indian Union in 1949, and we became Indian citizens once again.

Life in Calcutta was difficult for a refugee family from West Pakistan. It was difficult for a child of seven or eight to get admission to a good school without knowing any Bengali, English or Hindi (even if he did know Pashto and Urdu and Sindhi). Considering all these facts, my father took the decision to send me to a boarding school where I would be immersed in an environment of quick learning and be a settled soul for some years.

The school my father selected for my study was St Peter's Boys High School in Panchgani, about sixty miles from Poona. He chose this place, rather than sending me to one of the many good boarding schools in Darjeeling or nearer to Calcutta because my older cousin Hari Nain, son of the late Justice J L Nain, had been studying there for almost a year now and my father thought it would be best for me.

I went through life at Panchgani for eight years doing well in academics and sports like any other child and completed my Senior Cambridge. This was a typical British boarding school where everything was westernized. We had to dress for dinner, suited and booted, and eat with cutlery and crockery. Speaking in any language other than English was looked down upon. Our training was to become 'brown sahibs' – and I suppose it worked!

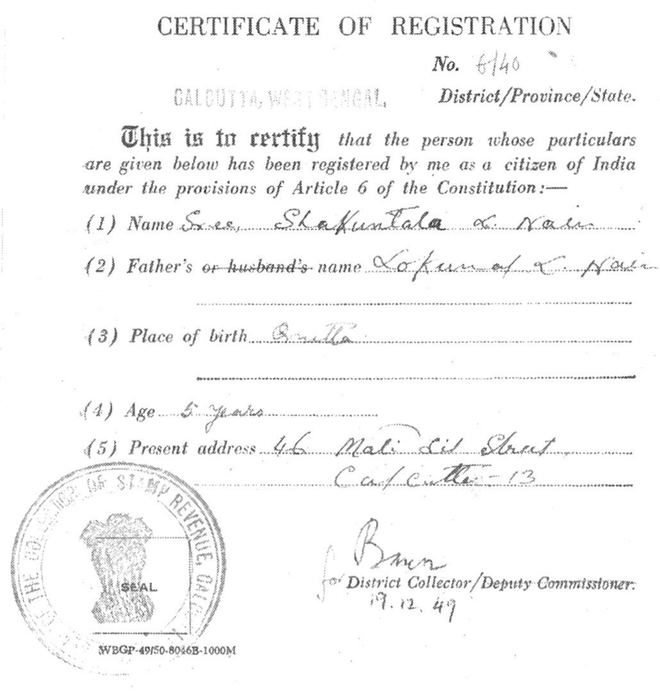

CERTIFICATE OF REGISTRATION

No. 6140

CALCUTTA, WEST BENGAL, *District/Province/State.*

This is to certify *that the person whose particulars are given below has been registered by me as a citizen of India under the provisions of Article 6 of the Constitution:—*

(1) Name Sree Shakuntala L Nain

(2) Father's ~~or husband's~~ name Lokumal L Nain

(3) Place of birth Quetta

(4) Age 5 years

(5) Present address 46 Mali Lil Street, Calcutta-13

SEAL

for *District Collector/~~Deputy Commissioner~~.*
17.12.49

WBGP-49/50-8046B-1000M

My certificate of registration as a citizen of India. I have often been interrogated at international airports about my current connections with Balochistan!

The journey that we survived

As narrated by my brother-in-law **Dr Jagdish Raisinghaney**

My grandfather Namomal Raisinghaney and my grandmother both passed away in 1920, leaving five small children. They were all brought up by different members of the extended family.

My father Jessasingh – the oldest among these five – was raised by a brother-in-law who stayed at Jacobabad, about thirty miles from Shikarpur and quite close to Sibi and Balochistan. Jacobabad was very hot in summer – and in winter, the temperatures dropped significantly. My father went to school in Jacobabad, and graduated from Aligarh University. He then got a job in Mithiana (Mithi) to teach English and Geography.

My father's youngest brother, Anand Ram, joined the army. We were at that time under British rule and he fought in the British army in Baghdad during the Second World War. After the war, things seemed to go well for some time, but then Partition was declared and riots started. It became imperative for us to leave Jacobabad.

The army brother had been given a posting to Fort William in Calcutta, and was permitted to take some members of the family with him. It was quickly decided that my parents and us children should leave with him, in the train reserved for army personnel. They would have to procure their own food at the stations where the train halted. I was just one or two years old.

My mother tells me that it was a very difficult journey and food was scarce. I was sick all the way. We went hungry most of the time. When the train stopped for a longish halt at a station, some of the males went out to procure food and milk for the children. At one stop, we were lucky to get some mutton. My mother prepared to wash and cook it. At last there would be a good meal! But while she was in the process of washing it, a monkey tried to pounce on her. She screamed and ran, trying to save herself, and it disappeared with the large chunks of the mutton. The family didn't get much to eat that day either.

At Kotri station, a bullet from a soldier's gun went off while he was cleaning it and killed a young Muslim boy. Pandemonium erupted and Hindu-Muslim riots broke out in a flash. Somehow, we were saved. On another occasion, a mob of Muslim rioters entered the train and came straight for my father. The train was carrying army personnel and had many Sikhs, who were the target of this attack. My father's name was Jessasingh, and they came to attack him. But seeing a frail-looking, well-educated man, caretaker of a large family with small children, they kept going, looking for another target. That day my father managed to save himself and us!

Many people on that train became sick with diarrohea and dysentery. We had no access to clean food or water throughout the journey. My parents have told me how much I suffered and how they were afraid I would not survive the journey. We were also scared to get off the train when it stopped because of the violence.

As soon as we reached the first station after crossing the new border, Ambala, there were celebrations. We felt we were home and safe. The first thing my parents did was to take me to a hospital for treatment ... and I survived!

How we pieced our lives together again

As narrated by my sister-in-law Mrs Raju Hari Nain

I spent my childhood in Rohri, Sindh. My father, Seth Hariram Hiranand Keswani, was a well-to-do businessman. His business interests were not just in Sindh but also in the south of India. He had invested money in Salem and Erode, where the rate of interest on hundi was higher than in Sindh. He had also established mills there to extract groundnut oil and remove chaff from rice. Along with his partners he also started a bus route, the Coimbatore Salem Transport Company.

In May 1947, just before Partition was announced, my father suffered a massive stroke and passed away at the young age of thirty-nine. Overnight, our lives changed. My mother suddenly had to take care of five children and her own old mother all on her own. We had to leave our well-furnished and comfortable home, and make arrangements to leave Pakistan. I was the youngest, just seven, and my brother Manohar, the eldest, was sixteen. It was a traumatic time but I remember everything so clearly, as my mother struggled to bear the burden of two tragedies: the sudden death of my father and Partition.

Some family members chartered a flight and flew with two of my brothers and my elder sister to Bombay. Rohri did not have an airport, so they had to drive in a jeep to Jacobabad. We were being watched. To avoid the attention of local authorities, they left at midnight. From Bombay they were taken to my masi's home in Jhansi, where her husband, Dr NJ Bakhru (FRCS) was District Medical Officer Central Railways.

The atmosphere was tense and depressing. My mother, grandmother, Manohar and I left our home and native place empty-handed to save ourselves, and travelled by train to Karachi. There we boarded the SS Dombra. and proceeded to Bombay, and from there to my masi's home in Jhansi. How relieved my mother was, to see her other three children safe and waiting for us there!

In 1948, we left for Bombay to continue our studies. My uncle, Dr Bakhru, arranged for us to stay at Central Railway Quarters near Kalyan railway station. After around three months, we shifted to a small rented house at Pherozeshah Mehta Road, and after eleven months we purchased a home in Dadar and moved in to it. Family members also booked some flats in Sion East, which they still own.

My eldest brother Manohar, the late Dr MH Keswani, became a plastic and reconstructive surgeon, and founded National Burns Centre in Airoli, Navi Mumbai.

We worked hard and got back on our feet

As narrated by my sister-in-law **Kanta Ashok Nain**

My parents were originally from Naushero, a small town near Karachi, and their journey started from there. They were recently married, and my mother was pregnant. With nothing but a wooden box containing clothes and utensils, and my mother's precious sewing machine, they left their home forever. On arrival in Delhi, all the refugees were herded into camps set up in the Old Fort. The living conditions were absolutely horrible with little or no sanitation. Thousands of people were crowded into one small area and they had to survive on limited rations and water supply. My brother Om was born in such a tent in Old Fort.

On our arrival in Delhi, my Nana immediately filed a claim for compensation. The compensation was given by the Government of India on the basis of the property he owned in Naushero. After much struggle, he was compensated with some land in Ramesh Nagar and Old Rajendra Nagar in Delhi.

Nana got the land, but this was just the beginning as there was no source of income. My mother, who was seventeen, was a matriculate, and my father, a graduate. Their education enabled them to apply for government positions and they both got jobs. Since Om was a baby, my nana and nani came to stay with us, so that they could look after him and manage the household while my parents were busy at work. Things slowly started falling into place. My parents would spend long hours at the office and would then come home and continue to work by lamplight. When they got possession of the land, they were able to construct a house on it. But during that time it was a struggle, and there were days when they barely had food to eat.

When we children hear these stories from our elders, we realize that though hardships never knock before coming, tough times do not last forever.

Shock followed shock, but we survived

As narrated by **Rukmani Chimanlal Balani** to her daughter Devika Sambhwani

I was eleven years old. Ours was a large joint family in Tando Adam. I remember very little of what happened, but one incident remains sharply etched in my mind. The family was talking about clashes between Sikhs and Muslims in Lahore. I didn't know where Lahore was and I thought it was some place a long distance away. But everyone in the family was very scared, and kept talking about killings and rivers of blood flowing.

Then one night a few days later, there was a loud banging on our doors. My parents, and my uncles and aunts and us siblings all huddled together in fear. Just as it seemed that they were on the verge of breaking down our doors, the police arrived and the crowd disappeared. Later I heard my parents saying that our Sindhi Muslim neighbour, God's good man, had saved us from the Muslim rioters by calling the police. We had been saved – but we were all traumatized. And now there was no choice, they said. It was time to leave.

The next day, I saw my mother packing food into a few boxes. I was surprised to see her packing gold coins and gold biscuits between the folded chapattis and ladoos! With tears in her eyes she told me that we would have to leave our homes, and that she was packing food for us for the journey.

We escaped on a train to Hyderabad, and had to wait

there for some time. Then, with the help of some friends, we reached Mirpur. The stress and anxiety affected my father so badly that he died. After that we were in shock, and travelled along with a group of Sindhis and just went wherever they went in a daze – to Marwar, and then to Udaipur. From one day to the next, we had no idea where our next destination was going to be.

I do remember a large bungalow in Udaipur. it belonged to a raja, and his retainer, seeing our sorry plight, let us camp there. There was a garden with fruits and vegetables, and it gave us our first meal after a long time. We left again and arrived in Ajmer. Many Sindhis were finding their way to Ajmer and we found ourselves following them. Ajmer became our home for some time. My uncles started an embroidery business with the 'claim' money we received. It was a paltry amount in comparison with the palatial house we had left behind in Tando Adam. But it was something.

At the age of sixteen I was married and we came and settled in Bombay and looked around for better prospects. My husband started a laundry business, but it was not successful. In the mean time, West End Hotel, which had been opened by Sindhis, offered him a job. Here he did well, and he was soon made Catering Officer. West End Hotel got the contract for catering to British Airways, and when Queen Elizabeth visited India, she travelled by British Airways. She was very impressed with the catering service and asked her to staff to write a letter of appreciation to West End Hotel and the Catering Officer. This brought us great happiness!

Adds Devika Sambhwani (daughter-in-law of IRB's masi):

> In spite of all the turmoil and hardships faced by my parents after Partition, they were able to give all of us a good education.

20. A summary of Sindhi history

By Dr Mira Raisinghaney, my sister

A generation which ignores history has no past and no future.

Robert Heinlein

In the 1920s, archaeologists and excavators made a startling discovery. An expedition under RD Banerji, an officer of the Archaeological Survey of India, chanced upon a mound of earth located west of the Indus River in Larkana District, Sindh. Sir John Marshall was Director General of the Archaeological Survey of India at the time, and he encouraged the excavations. It was a rich discovery, and led to the awareness of the antiquity of the history of Sindh.

Prudent urban planning and sanitary arrangements, thriving trade and commerce and all the amenities necessary to sustain a prosperous community: jewellery, clothes, artistic pottery, beautiful utensils and decorative glasses. The Sindhi expertise in trade and business, the hallmark of our community, was present even in our earliest ancestors, who travelled widely with their wares and had a thriving trade with Babylon, Mesopotamia and Egypt.

A single visit to the Chhatrapati Shivaji Maharaj Vastu Sangrahalaya in Mumbai, where a section is dedicated to the art and artefacts found at Mohen jo daro, will introduce the researcher to the glory that was Sindh. If only our leaders had had the foresight to save even a small part of our beloved motherland!

The Indus

The Indus river begins high up in the Himalayan mountains, the tallest mountain range in the world, and flows nearly 3000 kilometres to the Arabian Sea. As the river moves downstream it carves out a valley. This is where our ancestors settled.

Like everything else in Sindh, our Sindhu Nadi is unique, and its uniqueness lies in its wayward course. Ram Jethmalani, the eminent lawyer and politician called it 'poorali' – the whimsical one, pointing out that its varying channels obliterated historical evidence, and making it difficult to formulate an accurate picture of the past in Sindh.

The word 'Hindu' is derived from the Indo-Aryan and Sanskrit word 'Sindhu'. Meaning 'a large body of water', it was used as the name of the Indus River. When the Aryans, who were nature worshippers, came to India and saw the mighty banks of the river, perhaps they exclaimed in sheer wonder: "Sindhu!" India was originally called Sindhustan, or the land of the Sindhu and the Hindu. It is appropriate that the land should bear simply the name of the great river, for the river made it and nurtured it.

We read in the Ramayana that Sindh was part of Raja Dashrath's empire. When Rani Kaikeyi goes into a sulk, Dashrath tells her: "Sindh, Sauvira, Saurashtra, Anga, Vanga, Maghada, Kashi – all are mine. They produce an infinite variety of valuable articles. You can ask for whatever you like.

But, as we are told, Kaikeyi only wanted the throne for her son, Bharata.

Alexander in Sindh

Sindh is remembered for the visit of Sikander, Alexander of Macedonia (356-323 BC), who was known as a world conqueror. He is shown as the victor in his war with Porus. But Greek historians tell a different tale. According to them, Alexander actually fared badly against Porus in Punjab. The latter is said to have told him:

> Why should we make war with one another if you do not want to rob us of food and water? These are the only things wise men fight for. As for other possessions, I am ready to share them with you.

To which Alexander is said to have responded: "I shall do battle with you so far that however obliging you are, you shall not have the better of me."

In the battle, the Greeks were terrified of the Indian prowess, particularly intimidated by the war elephants, and they refused to fight. This demoralized Alexander so much that he not only allowed Porus to govern his own kingdom as satrap (representative of a ruler) but also some other kingdoms.

Life in Sindh was difficult for Alexander. When he saw the mighty Indus, he thought he had found the source of the Nile and with his much-depleted army, sailed down the river in the hope of reaching Egypt. However, with the advent of rain, his army became demoralized.

Alexander's adventures in Sindh were not totally unproductive. He introduced the Indian elephant to the West, as well as different varieties of spices and the mango. Delighted with the delicious mango, his men ate too many, which naturally led to loose motions, after which he forbade his people to eat mangoes.

One interesting thing the Greeks have in common with Sindhis is the *bŭja* – a gesture of denunciation, made with an out-stretched palm. When the Greek Cypriots wanted the British out of Cyprus, they burned the Union Jack and showed their retreating backs the Sindhi *bŭjo*!

Ashoka the Great

A decade after Alexander's invasion, Sindh witnessed the entry of Chandragupta Maurya in 313 BC. With him, Buddhism entered Sindh. The Buddhist city of Siraj-ji-takri is still located in the upper part of Sindh. It has visible ruins in the form of small mounds and other architectural remains that depict the presence of Buddhist culture. Hinduism too flourished at the same time and the two religions brought unity and stability to the country.

Emperor Ashoka, grandson of Chandragupta, is the most renowned king of the Mauryan Dynasty (322-185 BC). He was able to rule this vast empire initially through the precepts of the political treatise *Arthashastra*, attributed to the adviser and minister Chanakya, also known as Kautilya, who served Ashoka's father and grandfather. After his campaign against the Kingdom of Kalinga in 260 BC which resulted in rivers of blood and destruction, he renounced war, converted to Buddhism, and made Buddhism the state religion of India. Ashoka is remembered in history for the development of the concept of dhamma (pious social conduct).

Gautam Buddha (who died in 483 BC) was a prince and a warrior from a Kshatriya family and his influence left a permanent mark on Sindh; this influence is sometimes offered as an explanation of the nebulous caste system in Sindh.

The Kushans

With the weakening of the Mauryan Empire came the Kushans, a group of nomadic warriors from central Asia. From the first century to the third century of the millennium they ruled in the regions of northern India and Afghanistan. Emperor Kanishka was the greatest king of the Kushans, and he too played a vital role in the spread of Buddhism.

The Rai dynasty

The Rai Dynasty of Sindh (524–632) at its height ruled much of the North-Western regions of the Indian subcontinent. Their influence extended from Kashmir in the east, Makran and Debal ports (modern Karachi) in the west, Surat port in the south, and Kandahar. It covered an area of over 600,000 square miles, and reigned for a period of 143 years. The last ruler was Rai Sahasi the second.

The Brahman Dynasty

The Brahaman Dynasty which followed ruled briefly for not more than eighty or ninety years. After Rai Sahasi's death, his Brahman minister Chach usurped the throne and also married his widow, Suhandi. The *Chachnama* gives a detailed historical account of this Brahman dynasty and also records that the brother of Chach, Chander, was a devoted Buddhist and hence the remnants of several Buddhist monasteries can be seen in Sindh even today, particularly in the south. Chach was succeeded by his son Dahirsen, who was the last Hindu Raja of Sindh.

The robust tribes from the Northwest, with their strong and sturdy physique, were constantly swooping down on the civilized and tolerant people of the temperate zones. The geographical position of Sindh made her extremely vulnerable to attacks. The passes through the Kirthar range of mountains, which mark the boundary between Balochistan and Sindh, almost invited invaders.

Dahirsen had warded off several attacks by the Arabs but finally lost to Muhammad bin Qasim, an Arab commander of the Umayyad Caliphate who led the Muslim conquest of Sindh and Multan in the battle of Aror.

Over the next two centuries, more incursions came into Sindh: from the Sultans of Ghazni, then from the house of Ghor, the Khiljis, and the Tughlaqs. During the Tughlaq rule, Sindh was continually harassed by the inroads of rival factions and conversions. This led to the Hindus seeking succour in their religious beliefs.

Religion

Legend has it that a tyrannical ruler named Mirkhshah from nearby Thatta ordered the local Sindhis to convert to Islam within twenty-four hours. Fearful of this edict, the Sindhis prayed at the banks of the Indus, where they then saw a vision of the deity Varuna, who informed the worshippers that he would reincarnate himself as an infant to be born in Nasarpur in order to deliver them from their hardships. Jhulelal was born on the first day of the Hindu month of Chaitra. This day is celebrated by Sindhi Hindus as Cheti Chand. Sindhis all over the world greet one another with the words, *Jaiko chawando Jhulelal thenja thinde Beda Paar*

The teachings of Guru Nanak too influenced Sindhis as he travelled through Sindh and expounded his beautiful philosophy. His footwear can still be seen in the Gurdwara at Lakhpat (Kachchh). Sindhis worship Guru Nanak with the same fervour that they accord to Hindu gods.

The Moghuls and the Kalhoras

A new chapter started in Sindh with the arrival of the Moghuls, who changed the face of India with their political, military and artistic achievements.

Akbar, the greatest of the Moghul Emperors, was born in Umarkot, Sindh, and he reigned from 1556 to 1605. He extended his power over most of the Indian subcontinent, annexing Sindh to preserve the unity of his empire. The programs that he adopted won him the loyalty of both the Muslim and non-Muslim population of his realm. Sufism, a fine blend of Hinduism and Islam arrived through Kandahar and Multan, and blossomed. The Sindhis, liberal and peaceful and eclectic in their religious beliefs, accepted the teachings of the pirs with an open mind.

It is under the influence of the Sufi mystics that the poets of Sindh wove symbolic expressions and the vocabulary of wine and love into their poems and the Golden Period of Sindhi Literature shone brightly on the firmament. Art, literature, and music found a fertile ground to grow, and this came to full flowering in the early eighteenth century with the Muslim Kalhora dynasty.

During their reign flourished poets like Shah Abdul Latif Bhitai, Sachal, Sarmast, Sami and so many others.

Says Shah Abdul Latif:

> Though the forms of waves differ, water pervades them...

Sachal advises the fundamentalist mullas:

> O Mulla: taste the wine of God's love
> Otherwise go and hide your blackened face in a corner...

And Rohal's comment is true for all time:

> Religions have confused men of the world ...

The Talpurs

The Baluchi Talpur Mirs who came next were religious Muslims, but they were not intolerant. They built not only mosques but also Hindu temples, and attempted to rule peacefully. Beleaguered and harried by Sir Charles Napier under the instructions of Lord Ellenborough, Sindh was finally annexed to the British Empire in 1843.

Looking back through the ages, it is abundantly clear how constantly the history of Sindh has been determined by its geography. The political connections of Sindh have been mainly with the North and West, and communications with these regions have been far from easy as Sindh remained ruled for long periods by indigenous dynasties who entered through the mountain passes of the Northwest.

In 1947, India achieved independence from the British, after a long struggle and great sacrifices. Sindh became part of the newly-created Islamic state of Pakistan. Riots and violence erupted in Sindh. A massive exodus of Hindu Sindhis occurred and more than 1.1 million migrated to India. Most Sindhis have felt very strongly that we were betrayed by our own Sindhi Congress leaders. These political leaders made no attempt to save even a small part of Sindh for the Sindhi Hindus, while Punjab and Bengal were divided with parts allocated to both countries.

Through the centuries several dynasties made inroads into Sindh with their own customs and religious beliefs, and the Sindhis tolerantly absorbed the best of every culture, merging it with their own beliefs and traditions, never indulging in speech provoking war or aggressive behaviour. Also their relationship with the Muslims in pre-Partition times was always cordial and Popati Hiranandani expresses this beautifully when she says:

A Sindhi is a practising Hindu, a staunch believer

> in the vast Hindu pantheon worshipping Shiva, Rama, Krishna, Kali, Buddha, Guru Nanak, Varuna and all gods and saints and he won't forget his Muslim pir and will bow down in front of a holy dargah without any hesitation.

Clearly, the Partition of the country on religious lines was the most outrageous indignity to be perpetrated on a broad-minded, tolerant, liberal and accommodating people!

A NOTE TO THE READER

My generation – born in the mid-twentieth century – may be familiar with some of these stories and the nostalgia which our parents felt for their lost homeland Sindh. But later generations of Sindhis, scattered across the globe, will probably know very little about this ancestral homeland or how and why it was lost.

So in a nutshell: when the British Raj finally ended in 1947 following a long struggle by our patriots and nationalists, the dominion of India was divided. According to the Indian Independence Act of 1947 – an Act of British Parliament – India was divided into two independent dominions, India and Pakistan, with Lord Mountbatten as the first Governor General of Independent India and MA Jinnah as the first Governor General of Pakistan.

The dividing line to fix the international boundaries was drawn up by the Boundary Commission, chaired by Sir Cyril Radcliffe, a British lawyer who had no knowledge of India and who came to India for the first time on 8 July 1947 and had to complete the task in under six weeks. The boundary line cut through villages and at times even separated members of the same family. Radcliffe confessed years later to veteran journalist Kuldip Nayyar:

> I had no alternative; the time at my disposal was so short that I could not do a better job. Given the same period I would do the same thing. However, if I had two to three years, I might have improved on what I did.

It seems Radcliffe left India soon after the boundary line was declared as he envisaged that riots and bloodshed would follow and his own life was in jeopardy. And this was exactly what happened. The poet W H Auden, who is often referred to as the singular voice of a troubled age, responded to the absurdity of Partition and Radcliffe's daunting task in his poem *Partition*:

> But in seven weeks it was done, the frontiers decided,
> A continent for better or worse divided.
> The next day he sailed for England, where he quickly forgot
> The case, as a good lawyer must. Return he would not,
> Afraid, as he told his Club, that he might get shot.

Punjab and Bengal were divided into two parts: West Punjab and East Bengal became part of Pakistan. So Punjabis could migrate to East Punjab and Bengalis to West Bengal. But Sindh in its entirety became part of the Islamic state of Pakistan.

After the announcement of Independence at midnight on 14 August 1947, celebrations ensued on both sides of the border. But for Sindhi Hindus there was no celebration and singing. They had become homeless.

Events prior to 1947 had not given Sindhi Hindus any indication of the tragedy that was about to dawn on them. Assurances by Muslim leaders and their own political leaders had made them complacent. Moreover on the whole a spirit of cordiality existed between Hindus and their Muslim friends and neighbours who formed the majority community.

But events took a nasty turn with the arrival of Muslims from India whose eyes were directed towards taking possession of all that the affluent Hindu minority community possessed and had built up since generations. As AD Mani, editor of the Hitvada (a paper which had been started by India's patriot G K Gokhale and which flourished under the editorship of Mani) reported while on his way to Europe via Karachi :

"In Karachi I noticed signs of panic everywhere ... This was the one time beautiful city of Karachi where the Amils and Bhaibands had lent colour and richness to the aerial gateway of India. The powerful Bhaiband community have left en masse. Taking advantage of their world wide connections they have shifted their capital to Indian centres ... The Amils and Bhaibands have built Sindh brick by brick, stone by stone. With due respect to the Muslims of Sindh who have not been conspicuously successful ..."

Even Gandhi lamented that despite Jinnah's assurance to the minorities, communal violence and riots broke out and Sindhi Hindus were left with no choice but to leave everything and flee in order to save themselves, their women and their children. Over a million Hindu Sindhis fled in a short period of two to three months – by sea, bullock cart, train, whatever and wherever these migrants could manage to escape and survive.

The Government of India, still in its infancy and in the process of finding its own feet after Independence had been declared, organized makeshift refugee camps to accommodate the incoming hordes of refugees. My parents and us children were among these refugees who travelled from Karachi to Gujarat by SS Sonavati which was commissioned for evacuees leaving from Karachi.

It was the Sindhi community which rallied together and came forward with succour and support. Some Bhaiband Seths and Amil Sindhis already had homes in Bombay or were familiar with the city as Sindh had been part of Bombay Presidency after Sir Charles Napier's annexation of Sindh in 1843, and they went out of their way to help rehabilitate their suddenly displaced family and friends. Our enterprising Sindhworki and Shikarpuri mercantile communities who had been travelling since the 1800s to foreign lands for trading opportunities came forward to recruit salesmen and cashiers for their shops.

For Sindhis, the word diaspora has a special significance. The first disapora of Sindhis started in the middle of the nineteenth century when the adventurous business community sailed in search of trading markets. 'Musafiris' – the period of two to three years working in a different land – enabled them to become affluent and bring home wealth. With their spirit of philanthropy, they made donations to their home cities in Sindh for the building of schools, colleges, hospitals and rest houses. The second diaspora occurred when they were uprooted forcefully from their ancestral homes after Partition.

So if you are wondering, dear reader, why Sindhis are scattered across the globe – be it Tianjin or Yiwu or ShaoXing or Guangzhou or Kilwar or Kampala or Bushehr or Zanzibar or any other place unknown or unpronounceable by you – reasons are not far to seek. We are members of a scattered, adventurous and brave community.

I hope you have enjoyed journeying with me through our homeland – a place that we may never be able to actually go to.

Cheers!

Shakuntala Bharvani
Mumbai
February 2021

Acknowledgements

It takes a village to raise a child
African proverb

And it took a village to turn the idea of this book into reality. I want to acknowledge the people who helped make it happen.

1.Saaz Aggarwal, my editor and publisher, whom I cannot thank enough! She was the perfect partner with her deep knowledge of Sindh and efficient project plans which kept me on track. Her kindness and encouragement spurred me on at every step of this journey. No words are enough to thank you, Saaz.

2 Ashok Hinduja for his warm welcome when I visited him at Hinduja House. The photographs Ashish Ahuja provided gave me a chance to revisit past memories.

3. Anil Harish and Haresh Jagtiani for sharing their family stories and for always being like family to me.

4. My sister Mira Raisinghaney, a brilliant doctor who despite being younger than me, has always been an inspiration. I have been a struggler and an achiever because of the high bar she set.

5. My brothers Ashok and Ajit Nain who consider me the greatest sister in the world, after Mira (we are only two sisters). Their memories of Sindh have informed several anecdotes in this book.

6. Raju Nain, my sister-in-law, my mentor and my Sindhi Professor who energized me with her details and

remembrances of Rohri.

7. Susheel Harchandrai and Anil Bharvani, my two talented nephews who are so dear to me. You stepped forth graciously to help with photographs and sundry other materials. A big thank you.

8. And lastly, Vandana and Dhiren, who encouraged me to record these stories so that future generations of Sindhi children can learn about our heritage.

I hope to have done justice to the legacy of Sindhis around the world. While this book offers a limited set of stories, it is a testament to the fortitude, ingenuity and grit of a community that might have perished but continues to make its mark in the world.

About the author

Shakuntala Bharvani was awarded a 'First Class First' at the MA examination of Calcutta University in 1968. Having completed her doctoral thesis *Dorothy Richardson: Her Art and Technique as a Novelist* in 1973, she was selected by the Maharashtra Education Service, and started her career as Professor of English at Elphinstone College, Bombay, in 1973.

In 1985, Dr Bharvani was sponsored by the British Council to study at Exeter College, Oxford, and in 1990 was also a British Council Visitor to Downing College, Cambridge.

When English Language and Literature were introduced as compulsory subjects for Law students in 1996, she was transferred from Elphinstone College to the Government Law College, Bombay.

Her novel *Lost Directions* (Orient Longman, 1996) was a part of the Cultural Studies Programme at London University in 1999-2000.

In 2001, Dr Bharvani was selected for a Fulbright Teaching Program at City University of New York.

The *Law and Literature* (Himalaya Publishers, 2002), edited by her, has been a prescribed text for Law students at Bombay University since 2004. *Nissim Ezekiel, the Poet: A Monograph* (2004) was commissioned by the Sahitya Akademi.

Shakuntala Bharvani lives in Bombay – teaching, reading, and researching the history of Sindh.

Made in the USA
Las Vegas, NV
17 October 2021

32501234R10129